THE ESSENTIALS OF AI FOR BEGINNERS

A STEP-BY-STEP GUIDE TO GRASP AI CONCEPTS, STAY CURRENT WITH FUTURE TRENDS AND UNCOVER PRACTICAL APPLICATIONS

CAROLINE HYLANDS

CONTENTS

INTRODUCTION

I was out with a friend one evening not long ago. We had met up at a restaurant close to where we both live and to our amusement, a robot took our order and served our meal. It didn't look particularly life-like but executed the tasks with perfect efficiency. This certainly was a first for both of us and naturally, over dinner, my friend and I chatted about AI and how far it had come in the last few years. I had to admit I knew very little about it but I was AI-curious. As we got deeper into the conversation, it became clear that my friend knew a lot more about it than I did because of the books and articles she had read, as well as having done some online courses. That was when the world of AI started to open up in front of me, and my interest was sparked. I felt compelled to find out more. From that seed, the idea and motivation to write this book was born.

It is generally believed that AI is only for tech experts or that it's a force beyond our control. These misconceptions can make AI seem daunting. But AI is far from being an exclusive club or a rogue force. It's a tool that, when understood, can enhance our lives in many ways.

My primary goal is to make AI accessible to all. Whether you are a high school graduate, a college student, a professional in or out of the tech field, or a retiree, you can grasp AI concepts. You don't need a technical background to appreciate what AI can do or how it works. This book is your guide to understanding AI in a straightforward, relatable way and contains something for everyone.

The book is organized into several chapters, each building on the last. We start with the basics, explaining what AI is and how it came to be. Then, we move on to practical applications, showing how AI is used in many industries such as healthcare, finance, and entertainment. We also explore future trends, ethical considerations, and how AI impacts our daily lives. By the end, you'll have a well-rounded understanding of AI and its many facets.

Some simple, practical exercises are included, designed to help you understand the concepts while being fun and informative. For example, one exercise might involve using a simple AI app to recognize objects in photos, while another might guide you through creating a basic chatbot.

Understanding AI is crucial in today's world. AI is transforming industries, creating new job markets, and influencing our daily routines. For instance, AI algorithms are used in everything from recommending movies on streaming platforms to diagnosing diseases in healthcare. According to a recent study, AI will contribute around $15 trillion to the global economy by 2030. Having a knowledge of AI can help you stay current and competitive in a rapidly changing landscape.

Included is a glossary of standard terms to help you navigate the technical language of AI. This resource will make it easier for you to understand and engage with the material. You won't have to worry about getting lost in jargon, the glossary will be your handy reference guide.

While this book provides a solid foundation, it's just the beginning. AI is a vast and ever-evolving field and I encourage you to continue exploring beyond these pages. I have included resources and guidance for further learning, so you can dive deeper into the areas that interest you most.

It's important to dispel any fears or doubts you might have about AI, and my intention is to make this fascinating field accessible and enjoyable for everyone.

So, it's time to jump into the world of AI and find out how it can become an interest you can benefit from and have fun with. Let's get started!

1

UNDERSTANDING THE BASICS OF AI

On my way home one evening, I started thinking about how much technology has infiltrated our daily lives. For example, my car's navigation system, suggesting the fastest route to avoid traffic was once the stuff of science fiction. This system, an example of AI, was making decisions that saved me time and frustration. It's interesting when you contemplate how many people benefit from AI every day without thinking about it.

1.1 WHAT IS AI? DEMYSTIFYING THE BASICS

Artificial intelligence mimics human intelligence by imitating actions or decision-making processes. It involves building systems that handle tasks typically requiring human intelligence, like interpreting language recognizing patterns, solving problems, and making decisions. Think of AI as teaching a machine to think and learn from experiences, much like how a child learns. When a child learns to recognize a dog, they do so by seeing many examples and gradually understanding the common features. Similarly,

AI learns by processing vast amounts of data and identifying patterns.

Unlike traditional programming, where a programmer writes explicit instructions for a computer to follow, AI systems learn from data. Traditional programming is like giving a precise recipe to a chef, specifying every step. AI, on the other hand, is like teaching the chef cooking techniques and letting them create dishes based on what they've learned. This ability to learn and adapt makes AI incredibly powerful and versatile.

AI is already part of our daily lives. For example, virtual assistants like Siri and Alexa use AI to understand and respond to your voice commands. When you ask Siri for the weather or Alexa to play a song, they process your request, search for the information and provide an accurate response. Similarly, recommendation engines on platforms like Netflix and Amazon use AI to suggest movies and products you might like based on your past behavior. These systems analyze your viewing or shopping history and predict your preferences, making your experience more personalized and enjoyable.

Another fascinating application is autonomous vehicles like Tesla cars. These vehicles use AI to navigate roads, avoid obstacles, and make real-time driving decisions. They process data from cameras, sensors and GPS to understand their surroundings and ensure a safe journey. In healthcare, AI-powered diagnostic tools assist doctors in identifying diseases from medical images, improving accuracy and speed in diagnosis. These examples show how AI enhances convenience, safety and efficiency in various aspects of life.

It's important to understand the different types of AI to appreciate its capabilities and limitations. Narrow AI, also known as weak AI, is designed to perform specific tasks like playing chess or filtering spam emails. These systems excel at their designated functions but cannot perform tasks outside their programmed domain. For instance, a chess-playing AI cannot suddenly start diagnosing medical conditions. On the other hand, General AI or strong AI refers to systems capable of performing any intellectual task that a human can do. These systems can understand, learn, and apply knowledge across various fields. While narrow AI is prevalent today, general AI remains a concept for the future, representing a significant leap in AI capabilities.

Common misconceptions about AI often stem from its portrayal in movies and media. Many people think AI is synonymous with robots possessing consciousness and emotions. In reality, AI systems do not have feelings or self-awareness. They process data and make decisions based on algorithms and patterns, not emotions. This is a good thing because who needs emotional AI? Another myth is that AI is infallible. However, AI systems can make errors, especially if they are trained on biased or incomplete data. Understanding these nuances helps us appreciate AI for what it truly is, a powerful tool designed to assist and enhance human capabilities, not replace them.

1.2 THE EVOLUTION OF AI: FROM TURING TO TODAY

The story of AI begins with Alan Turing, a mathematician and logician whose work laid the groundwork for modern computing and AI. In 1950, Turing proposed the idea of a machine that could simulate any human intelligence task, a concept he explored in his famous paper "Computing Machinery and Intelligence." He introduced the Turing Test, a measure of a machine's ability to exhibit human-like intelligence. The test involved a human judge engaging in conversation with both a human and a machine designed to generate human-like responses. If the judge could not reliably distinguish the machine from the human, the machine was considered to have passed the test. This idea of creating machines that can think like humans was revolutionary and set the stage for future AI research.

A pivotal moment in AI history occurred in 1956 at the Dartmouth Conference, organized by John McCarthy, Marvin Minsky, Nathaniel Rochester, and Claude Shannon. The attendees of this pivotal conference were optimistic about the potential of AI, believing that machines could be built to simulate any aspect of human intelligence. They set ambitious goals and laid the foundation for AI research, but the journey was challenging. The field experienced several "AI winters," periods when funding and interest in AI research waned due to unmet expectations and slow progress. These setbacks were frustrating, but they also led to important reflections and re-evaluations of AI approaches.

Despite these challenges, AI continued to advance, reaching significant milestones that captured public attention. One such milestone was IBM's Deep Blue defeating chess grandmaster Garry Kasparov in 1997. This victory was a testament to the power of AI in mastering complex tasks that required strategic thinking. Another breakthrough came in 2016 when Google's AlphaGo defeated Go champion Lee Sedol 4-1 in a 5-game match. Go is a board game known for its complexity and intuition-based strategies, making AlphaGo's victory a significant achievement in AI. These successes were made possible by advances in neural networks and deep learning, which allowed machines to learn and improve their performance over time.

As AI evolved, its impact on technology and society became increasingly evident. The development of personal computing and the internet revolutionized how we live and work, and AI played a crucial role in these advancements. In robotics and automation, AI-enabled the creation of machines that could perform tasks with precision and efficiency, transforming industries like manufacturing and logistics. In medicine, AI-powered tools improve diagnostic accuracy and personalized treatment plans. In finance, AI algorithms enhanced fraud detection and optimized trading strategies. The entertainment industry saw AI-driven recommendation systems that customized user experiences, making it easier for people to discover new content they loved.

Looking ahead, the future of AI holds exciting possibilities. Quantum computing which employs the principles of quantum mechanics, promises to increase computational power exponentially, enabling more complex AI models and faster problem-solving. In space exploration, AI can assist in autonomous navigation, data analysis and mission planning, pushing the boundaries of what we can achieve beyond Earth. However, with these advancements come ethical and societal implications that must be addressed. The potential for AI to impact jobs, privacy, and decision-making requires careful consideration and responsible development to ensure that AI benefits all of humanity.

1.3 KEY AI TERMINOLOGIES SIMPLIFIED

Understanding the vocabulary of Artificial Intelligence is like learning a new language. I have included a glossary of terms but here are a few to get you started.

Machine learning is a subset of AI that involves training computers to learn from data using algorithms and models to make decisions or predictions. Suppose you want to teach a computer to recognize different breeds of dogs. You'd feed it thousands of images of various breeds, and by analyzing patterns and features, it would learn to identify them. Machine learning drives many AI applications, from recommendation systems to fraud detection.

Deep learning takes machine learning a step further by using neural networks, which are inspired by the human brain, consisting of layers of interconnected neurons. Each layer processes a part of the input data, passing the refined output to the next layer. Picture a neural network like a series of sieves, each filtering out more impurities until only the purest substance remains. This process allows deep learning models to handle complex tasks such as image and speech recognition. For instance, self-driving cars use deep learning to interpret their surroundings and make driving decisions.

Algorithms are the step-by-step instructions AI systems follow to perform tasks. Think of an algorithm as a recipe. Just as a recipe guides a chef through the process of cooking a dish, an algorithm guides a computer through solving a problem. Some algorithms are simple, like sorting a list of numbers, while others are complex, like predicting stock market trends. Data science involves studying data to find patterns and insights, much like a detective solving a mystery. Data scientists collect, clean, and analyze data to help AI models learn and make accurate predictions.

Big data refers to the vast amounts of data generated daily from various sources, including social media, sensors, and transactions which is essential for training AI models. To handle big data, we need powerful tools and techniques to store, process, and analyze it efficiently.

Natural Language Processing (NLP) is a field within AI that enables machines to understand and interpret human language. NLP powers applications like chatbots, language translation services, and voice assistants. Imagine talking to a friend who speaks a different language and having an interpreter instantly translate your conversation. That's what NLP does but with text and speech.

Computer vision is another branch of AI that allows machines to analyze and interpret visual data. Computer vision applications include facial recognition, object detection and medical image analysis. For example, when you upload a photo to Facebook, computer vision algorithms help you tag your friends automatically.

Understanding these terms in context helps grasp the broader AI landscape. Familiarizing yourself with these key terminologies will better equip you to navigate the world of AI and appreciate its potential.

1.4 THE AI ECOSYSTEM: ROLES AND COMPONENTS

To understand the AI ecosystem, it's essential to break down its main components. At the core of any AI system is data. Data is the foundation, providing the raw material that AI algorithms need to learn and make decisions. Data is like engine fuel. Without it, the engine can't run. Every interaction, transaction and piece of digital information contributes to this vast pool of data. From social media posts to medical records, data is collected, cleaned and prepared for use in AI models.

Algorithms are the next critical component. These are the rules and processes that guide AI in making sense of the data. Think of algorithms as the recipes that turn raw ingredients into a finished dish. They take the data and process it in a way that allows the AI to identify patterns, make predictions, and generate insights. Different algorithms serve different purposes. Some are designed for classification tasks, such as determining whether an email is spam, while others are used for regression tasks, like predicting housing prices.

The third essential element is computing power. This refers to the hardware and software that run AI models. High-performance processors, graphics processing units (GPUs), and specialized AI chips provide the computational resources to handle large datasets and complex algorithms. Cloud services like AWS and Google Cloud offer scalable computing power, enabling developers to build and deploy AI models without investing in expensive hardware. These platforms provide the infrastructure that supports the intensive computations required for AI tasks.

Within the AI ecosystem, various roles contribute to the development and application of AI. Data scientists are responsible for collecting, analyzing and interpreting data. They clean and preprocess the data to ensure it's suitable for training AI models. Machine learning engineers build and optimize these models. They select appropriate algorithms, train the models and fine-tune them to achieve the best performance. AI researchers advance the theoretical understanding of AI, exploring new algorithms and techniques to expand the limits of what AI can do. AI ethicists address the moral and societal concerns associated with AI, ensuring that AI systems are developed and used responsibly.

AI projects require collaboration across different domains. Domain experts provide insights into the specific problem being addressed, while technologists bring expertise in AI and data science. For instance in healthcare, doctors and medical researchers work with data scientists and machine learning engineers to develop diagnostic tools. Teamwork is crucial in data collection and model training, ensuring the AI system is built on accurate and relevant information. Feedback loops from end-users play a vital role in refining AI models, as real-world use can reveal areas for improvement.

Several tools and platforms facilitate AI development. Python is a popular programming language due to its simplicity and extensive libraries. TensorFlow and PyTorch are widely used frameworks for building and training AI models. They provide the tools necessary to create complex neural networks and deep learning models. Jupyter Notebooks offer an interactive coding environment, allowing developers to write and run code, visualize data, and document their work all in one place. AWS and Google Cloud provide the infrastructure and computing power to handle large-scale AI projects.

The combination of these components and roles forms a dynamic and interconnected ecosystem. Each part plays a crucial role in the development and application of AI, contributing to its growth and evolution. Understanding this ecosystem helps demystify AI and reveals the collaborative efforts behind every AI system.

1.5 HOW AI LEARNS: AN OVERVIEW OF MACHINE LEARNING

Machine learning is the bedrock of modern artificial intelligence. It revolves around the principle that machines learn from data, identify patterns, and make decisions with minimal human input. AI learns from large datasets, identifying patterns and making predictions.

The process begins with training data, which is a collection of examples that the AI system learns from. These examples include inputs (like images or text) and corresponding outputs (like labels or categories). The AI system analyzes this data to find patterns and relationships. Next are the validation and test datasets. While the training data teaches the AI, the validation data helps fine-tune the model, ensuring it generalizes well to new data. The test dataset evaluates the model's performance, providing an unbiased assessment of its accuracy and reliability.

Machine learning can be categorized into three main types: supervised, unsupervised, and reinforcement. In supervised learning, the AI system learns from labeled data. Each training example has a label that tells the AI the correct output. For example, if you're training an AI to recognize handwritten digits, each image in the training set is labeled with the corresponding digit. The AI learns to map inputs to outputs by finding patterns in the data. This method is widely used in applications like spam detection, where emails are labeled as "spam" or "not spam," and the AI learns to classify new emails accordingly.

Unsupervised learning, on the other hand, deals with unlabeled data. The AI system must find patterns and structures within the data without any guidance on what the outputs should be. Imagine sorting a box of mixed fruit without knowing any names or categories. You might group them by color, size, or shape. Similarly, the AI groups data points based on similarities. Clustering and association are common techniques in unsupervised learning. For instance, in market basket analysis, unsupervised learning helps identify products frequently bought together, enabling retailers to optimize their inventory and marketing strategies.

Reinforcement learning is akin to how we learn from trial and error. The AI system interacts with an environment, takes actions, and receives feedback through rewards or penalties. Over time it learns to maximize the rewards by choosing the best actions. Think of teaching a dog to fetch a ball. The dog explores various actions, and when it successfully brings the ball back, it receives a treat (reward). In AI, reinforcement learning is used in applications like game playing, where the system learns to develop winning strategies by playing the game repeatedly and learning from its successes and failures.

The machine learning process involves several steps. It starts with data collection and preprocessing. Raw data is gathered from various sources and cleaned to remove errors and inconsistencies, ensuring the data is suitable for training. Next is model selection and training. The AI system selects an appropriate algorithm and uses the training data to build a model. The model can then make predictions by adjusting its parameters to minimize errors. This process is iterative, with the model continuously refining itself.

When the model is trained, it undergoes evaluation and tuning. The validation dataset helps fine-tune the model, ensuring it performs well on new, unseen data. Metrics like accuracy, precision and recall assess the model's performance. If necessary, the model is adjusted to improve its results. Finally, the model is deployed and monitored. It is integrated into real-world applications, where it makes predictions and decisions. Continuous monitoring ensures the model remains accurate and relevant, adapting to changes in data and requirements.

Practical examples of machine learning abound. In email services, spam detection algorithms analyze incoming emails for patterns associated with spam, filtering them out before they reach your inbox. Social media platforms use image recognition to automatically tag friends in photos, enhancing user experience by identifying faces and objects. In finance, predictive analytics models forecast stock prices, helping investors make informed decisions. E-commerce platforms employ personalization algorithms to recommend products based on your browsing and purchase history, making shopping more enjoyable and efficient.

With a clear understanding of how AI learns, it becomes evident that machine learning is not just a theoretical concept but a practical tool with vast applications. It bridges the gap between data and actionable insights, transforming industries and improving our daily lives. By grasping these foundational principles, you are better equipped to appreciate the power of AI and its potential to drive innovation and progress.

2

MASTERING PROMPTS: THE KEY TO UNLOCKING AI'S POTENTIAL

I n AI, a prompt is like a key: it unlocks specific responses from the system and the better the key fits, the smoother the door opens. As I have learned, there's far more to prompting than meets the eye, and some thought and creativity are required to get the best result.

2.1 WHAT ARE PROMPTS?

A prompt serves as an instruction that guides the AI to generate specific responses. Think of a prompt as a command you give to a very sophisticated digital assistant. Just like a teacher provides a student with a question to answer, a prompt gives the AI a task to complete. These tasks can range from generating text, interpreting data, to even simulating a customer service response. The quality of the prompt directly influences the quality of the AI's output, making it crucial to frame your instructions clearly and effectively.

Prompts are the bridge between your intent and the AI's comprehension. When you provide a prompt, you're essentially telling the

AI what you want it to do. For instance, if you're using an AI tool to draft a blog post, your prompt might include the topic, key points, and the desired tone. The AI then processes this information and generates content that aligns with your instructions. The clearer and more detailed your prompt, the better the AI can understand and deliver a relevant response.

Prompts come in various forms, each suited to different types of AI interactions. Text prompts are perhaps the most common. These are written instructions that guide the AI to generate text-based responses. For example if you're using a content creation tool, you might provide a prompt like "Write a persuasive email to potential clients about our new product." The AI will then generate an email based on your instructions, considering the persuasive tone and the topic of the new product.

Voice prompts are another type, especially prevalent in virtual assistants like Siri and Alexa. When you say, "Alexa, play some relaxing music" you're giving a voice prompt. The AI processes your spoken words, understands the request and plays music that fits the relaxing genre. Voice prompts are particularly useful for hands-free interactions, making them popular in smart home devices and mobile assistants.

Image prompts guide AI systems to generate or interpret visual content. For instance, when using an AI-driven design tool, you might upload an image and provide a prompt like, "Enhance the colors and add a vintage filter." The AI analyzes the image and applies the specified edits. Image prompts are widely used in photo editing applications, graphic design tools, and even in creating AI-generated artworks.

Across various AI platforms, prompts play a pivotal role. In chatbots, prompts help simulate human-like conversations. A customer service chatbot might use prompts to generate responses to customer inquiries, making the interaction seamless and efficient. In AI-driven content creation tools, prompts guide the AI to produce articles, social media posts and other written content. By providing detailed prompts, you can ensure the AI generates content that meets your specific needs and expectations.

Understanding the different types of prompts and their applications is the first step in mastering AI interactions. Whether you're drafting a text prompt for a writing tool, issuing a voice command to a virtual assistant, or guiding an image editing AI, the principles remain the same. Clear, specific prompts lead to better, more relevant outputs, enhancing your overall experience with AI. In the next sections, we'll delve deeper into crafting effective prompts, addressing common challenges, and optimizing interactions for the best possible results.

2.2 CRAFTING EFFECTIVE PROMPTS

When it comes to constructing effective AI prompts, clarity and precision are paramount. Imagine asking your AI to "generate an image of a cat." This prompt is vague and leaves much to the AI's interpretation. The result could range from a cartoon cat to a photographic image, and the cat could be in any setting. Now, consider a more precise prompt: "Generate an image of a tabby cat sitting on a windowsill." This prompt provides specific details, guiding the AI to produce a more accurate and relevant image. The added specificity helps the AI understand exactly what you want, reducing the chances of generating a less useful response.

Clarity in prompts eliminates ambiguity, which is crucial for achieving desired outcomes. When a prompt is ambiguous, the AI has to guess your intent, often leading to unexpected results. For example, if you ask an AI to "write a story about a hero," the result could be a superhero tale, a historical account, or even a fantasy adventure. By specifying, "write a short story about a firefighter hero saving a cat from a tree," you provide a clear direction, ensuring the AI's output aligns with your expectations. The more precise and clear your prompts are, the better the AI can meet your needs.

Contextual awareness plays a significant role in shaping AI responses. Providing context within your prompts can lead to more accurate and nuanced outputs. Consider the difference between "summarize this article" and "summarize this article for a 10-year-old." The latter prompt adds a layer of complexity, instructing the AI to tailor the summary to a younger audience. This additional context helps the AI adjust its language and explanation style, making the summary more appropriate and understandable for a child. Context helps the AI grasp the subtleties of your request, enhancing the relevance of its response.

Effective prompting involves understanding the context in which the AI operates. For instance, when using an AI to generate a marketing email, providing background information about the target audience, the product, and the campaign goals can make a significant difference. A prompt like "create a marketing email for our new eco-friendly water bottle" is a good start. However, adding context such as "aimed at environmentally conscious college students, highlighting its sustainability features and affordability" gives the AI a clearer picture of your expectations. This context enables the AI to craft a message that resonates with the intended audience.

To illustrate further, let's consider using AI for customer service. A prompt like "generate a response to a customer complaint" is quite broad. Providing context such as "generate a polite and empathetic response to a customer complaint about delayed shipping, offering a discount on their next purchase" helps the AI understand the situation better. The response will likely be more aligned with your customer service standards, addressing the specific issue and offering a solution that enhances customer satisfaction.

A big plus is that crafting effective prompts also allows for iteration and refinement. This means that sometimes, your initial prompt might not give the desired result. It's comforting to realise that in such cases, all is not lost and by refining the prompt and adding more details or rephrasing you can improve the output. For example, if you start with "generate a blog post about healthy eating," and the result is too general, you might refine it to "generate a blog post about healthy eating tips for busy professionals, focusing on quick and nutritious meals." This refinement provides the AI with a clearer direction, leading to a more useful and targeted blog post.

By focusing on clarity, precision and context, you can craft prompts that guide the AI to produce accurate and relevant responses. Whether you're generating content, interpreting data, or simulating customer interactions, well-crafted prompts are the key to unlocking the full potential of AI.

2.3 COMMON CHALLENGES AND SOLUTIONS

When crafting AI prompts, ambiguity often arises as a common challenge. Ambiguous prompts leave too much room for interpretation, leading to outputs that miss the mark. You could instruct an AI to "Write a letter." but this prompt is open-ended, and the AI might write anything from a personal note to a business proposal. To avoid this, you need to be descriptive and specific. Adding qualifiers and constraints helps. For instance, "Write a formal business letter to a potential customer introducing our new software product" provides clear guidance. This specificity ensures that the AI understands the context, audience, and purpose, resulting in a more relevant response.

Another frequent issue is over-complexity in prompts. When prompts are too detailed or intricate, the AI can become confused, producing muddled or less effective responses. Think of trying to explain a complicated recipe in one breath, versus breaking it down into steps. The same applies to AI prompts. Instead of asking, "Create a detailed marketing plan outlining our social media strategy, email campaigns, and influencer partnerships for the next quarter," break it down. Start with, "Outline a social media strategy for the next quarter." Once you have that, move on to, "Draft a plan for our email campaigns," and so forth. This sequential approach simplifies the task, enabling the AI to focus on one aspect at a time, leading to clearer and more useful outputs.

Unintended bias is another challenge that can slip into prompts unnoticed. Biases can skew AI responses, leading to outputs that may not be fair or inclusive. For example, if you prompt an AI to "Generate a list of top CEOs," and it only lists men, there may be an underlying bias in the data or the way the prompt is phrased. To avoid this, use neutral and inclusive language. Instead of "Generate a list of top CEOs," specify, "Generate a list of top CEOs, ensuring diversity in gender and ethnicity." This directive encourages the AI to consider a broader spectrum of candidates, reducing the likelihood of biased outputs. Awareness of how prompts can inadvertently introduce bias is crucial in crafting fair and balanced instructions.

When dealing with ambiguity, over-complexity, and unintended bias, iterative refinement of prompts is key. Start with a basic prompt and gradually add layers of detail and context. Monitor the AI's responses and tweak the prompts as necessary to achieve the desired results. For instance, if your initial prompt, "Write a blog post about healthy eating," results in a generic article, refine it to, "Write a blog post about healthy eating tips for college students on a budget." This refinement process helps in honing the AI's focus and ensuring the output aligns with your expectations.

Understanding the AI's capabilities and limitations is also essential. Not all AI systems have the same level of sophistication or access to the same datasets. Tailoring your prompts to the strengths of the specific AI tool you are using can significantly improve the quality of the responses. For example, if you're using an AI known for its language processing abilities, leverage that strength by providing detailed and context-rich prompts. Conversely, if the AI excels in data analysis, focus your prompts on tasks that involve interpreting and summarizing data.

By addressing these common challenges and implementing thoughtful solutions, you can craft prompts that lead to more accurate, relevant, and fair AI responses. This approach not only enhances the effectiveness of your AI interactions but also ensures that the outputs are aligned with your goals and values.

2.4 OPTIMIZING PROMPTS FOR BETTER AI INTERACTION

When refining prompts to get the best out of AI, focusing on clarity and simplicity can make a significant difference. Using the active voice makes your instructions direct and easy to understand. For instance, instead of saying, "A summary of the document should be provided," you might say, "Summarize the document." This straightforward approach guides the AI more effectively. Avoiding jargon is equally important. AI algorithms can get confused by specialized or technical terms that are not universally understood. If you need the AI to draft an email, it's better to say, "Write an email to a client explaining our new product," rather than using complex business terms.

Including examples within your prompt further clarifies your expectations. Suppose you want the AI to generate a persuasive email. You could say, "Write a persuasive email to a potential client about our new product. For example, 'Our latest innovation offers a 20% increase in efficiency, saving you both time and money.'" This example gives the AI a clear template to follow, reducing the likelihood of vague or off-target responses. By providing specific examples, you help the AI understand the tone, structure, and key points you want to include.

Feedback is a powerful tool in optimizing prompt creation. When you use an AI system, it's crucial to analyze the responses it generates. This analysis can reveal patterns and areas where the AI might not be aligning with your expectations. For instance, if you notice that the AI consistently generates overly formal text when you want a casual tone, you can adjust your prompts accordingly. Instead of "Write a letter to a friend," you might refine it to, "Write a casual letter to a friend, using a friendly and relaxed tone."

Iterating on your prompts based on feedback allows for continuous improvement. Start with a basic prompt and see what the AI produces. If the output isn't quite right, tweak the prompt by adding more details or changing the wording. This iterative process helps fine-tune the AI's responses to better match your needs. For example, if your initial prompt, "Draft a report on quarterly sales," results in a dry and data-heavy document, you might revise it to, "Draft a concise and engaging report on quarterly sales, highlighting key trends and insights."

Refinement techniques also involve using constraints and qualifiers to guide the AI. If you want the AI to generate a response within a specific context, include that context in your prompt. For instance, "Generate a press release about our new product launch, emphasizing its eco-friendly features and targeting environmentally conscious consumers." This directive ensures that the AI focuses on the aspects that matter most to you, leading to a more relevant and effective output.

By continuously refining your prompts and using feedback to guide improvements, you can optimize your interactions with AI. This process not only enhances the accuracy and relevance of the AI's responses but also makes your experience with AI tools more productive and satisfying.

2.5 PRACTICAL APPLICATIONS

Effective prompting can transform how you interact with AI across various real-world scenarios. In content creation, well-crafted prompts enable AI to generate interesting well-written articles, social media posts, and marketing materials.

In customer service, prompts guide AI to provide accurate and helpful responses to customer inquiries. For example, AI can be used by online retailers to handle common customer questions about order status, returns, and product information. By crafting prompts like "create a response for a customer who wants information about the status of their order, including estimated delivery time and tracking information," the AI can generate clear and informative replies. This reduces the workload on human customer service team and ensures customers receive timely assistance.

For personal productivity, AI can act as a virtual assistant, managing tasks and organizing schedules. Say you need to draft a to-do list for a busy week. A prompt like "generate a weekly to-do list including work meetings, grocery shopping, exercise routines and family commitments" helps the AI create a comprehensive plan. You then have more time to complete tasks rather than having to organize them.

Case studies offer valuable insights into the effectiveness of well-crafted prompts.

For example, a university employed AI to assist in grading student essays. The initial prompts were simple, such as "grade this essay." However, these prompts didn't account for the nuances of different grading criteria. By refining the prompts to include specific guidelines like "evaluate this essay based on clarity, argument strength, grammar, and adherence to the topic," the AI provided more accurate and consistent grades. This allowed professors to focus on providing qualitative feedback, resulting in a better learning experience for students.

These examples underscore the importance of effective prompting in maximizing AI's potential. By carefully crafting your prompts, you can ensure that the AI understands your intentions and delivers high-quality outputs. This enhances efficiency and productivity and allows you to leverage AI in innovative ways across various aspects of your life and work.

3

DIVING DEEPER INTO MACHINE LEARNING

I t's a long time since I noticed for the first time that an email had automatically been sorted into my spam folder, something I now take for granted. The accuracy with which my email service could distinguish between unwanted messages and important communications seemed as though it should be impossible. This convenience is made possible by supervised learning, a fundamental concept in machine learning. Let's explore supervised learning, how it works and how it differs from unsupervised learning.

3.1 SUPERVISED VS. UNSUPERVISED LEARNING: WHAT'S THE DIFFERENCE?

Supervised learning uses labeled data to train models for predicting outcomes or classifications. Suppose you have a stack of emails, each labeled as "spam" or "not spam." The job of supervised learning is to teach the model to recognize patterns in the labeled data to correctly classify new, unlabeled emails. This process involves feeding the model examples of both spam and non-spam emails, along with their labels, so it can learn to identify the features that distinguish one from the other. Over time, the model becomes proficient at sorting emails based on these learned patterns.

In supervised learning, labeled datasets play a crucial role. These datasets consist of input-output pairs, where the input is the data fed into the model, and the output is the label associated with that data. For example, in image recognition, the input might be a photo, and the output could be a label indicating whether the photo contains a cat or a dog. The model uses these examples to learn how to map inputs to outputs, to make accurate predictions on new data. This method is widely used in various applications, such as predicting stock prices, diagnosing medical conditions and even recognizing faces in photo libraries.

On the other hand, unsupervised learning is when algorithms analyse and identify patterns in unlabeled data. Instead of being told what to look for, the model must find patterns and relationships in the data independently. Think of it as exploring a new city without a map. You wander through the streets, gradually noticing which areas are similar and which ones are different. In marketing, unsupervised learning is often used for customer segmentation. By analyzing purchasing behaviors, the model can group customers into various segments based on their similarities, even though it doesn't know the specific characteristics of each group. This helps businesses tailor their marketing strategies to different customer segments more effectively.

Clustering algorithms like K-means are key tools in unsupervised learning. K-means works by dividing data points into clusters based on their similarities. It will identify clusters of customers who exhibit similar behaviors, such as purchasing the same types of products or visiting the same store locations. This method is also useful in anomaly detection, where the object is to find unusual patterns that deviate from the norm. For example, in fraud detection, unsupervised learning can help spot suspicious transactions that don't fit a customer's typical spending patterns.

Supervised learning is highly effective for tasks like classification and regression. For instance, forecasting house prices based on features like location, size, and number of bedrooms is a typical supervised learning task. In contrast, unsupervised learning is ideal for exploring and identifying hidden patterns within large datasets. It excels in tasks like clustering and association, where the goal is to uncover relationships and structures in the data.

Let's illustrate these concepts with real-world case studies. In manufacturing, predictive maintenance is a common application of supervised learning. By analyzing data of performance and maintenance records, the model can predict when a machine is likely to fail, allowing for timely maintenance and reducing downtime, which saves costs and enhances productivity. In retail, market basket analysis is a classic example of unsupervised learning. By examining transaction data, the model can identify products that are frequently bought together. This insight helps retailers optimize product placements and create targeted promotions, boosting sales and customer satisfaction.

Understanding the differences and applications of supervised and unsupervised learning is crucial for leveraging the power of machine learning. By selecting the appropriate approach based on the nature of your data and the problem you're trying to solve, you can harness the full potential of these techniques to drive innovation and efficiency in various fields.

3.2 NEURAL NETWORKS EXPLAINED: THE HUMAN BRAIN ANALOGY

Neural networks are another interesting aspect of AI, mirroring the structure and function of the human brain. Picture your brain's neurons, tiny cells that transmit information through electrical and chemical signals. In a neural network, these neurons are replaced by nodes. Each node processes a piece of information, much like a neuron does. A neural network consists of three layers, namely the input, hidden, and output layer. The input layer receives the raw data, which is then processed through one or more hidden layers before reaching the output layer, where the final prediction or decision is made. This layered approach allows neural networks to handle complex tasks by breaking them down into more manageable steps.

Understanding how neural networks learn involves diving into forward and backward propagation processes. Forward propagation is the initial step, where data moves through the network from the input, through to the hidden layers and lastly to the output layer. Think of it as flowing water through a series of pipes, each representing a layer in the network. At each node, the input data is multiplied by a set of weights. The weights refer to the strength of the connections between the nodes. The data is then summed up, and an activation function is applied to give an output. This output then becomes the input for the next layer. The ultimate goal is to produce an output that closely matches the desired result. However, the first attempt is rarely perfect, leading us to backward propagation.

Backward propagation, or backward propagation of errors has the purpose of error correction. It involves the adjusting of the weights based on the error in the output so that a more accurate final output is achieved. This step is crucial for improving the network's accuracy. Imagine you're learning to throw a basketball into a hoop. If you miss, you adjust your aim based on the error. Similarly, backward propagation adjusts the weights in the network to minimize the error. The error is calculated by comparing the network's output to the actual target. This error is then propagated back through the network, layer by layer, adjusting the weights to reduce the error in future iterations. This iterative process continues until the network's output is sufficiently accurate.

Activation functions play a vital role in neural networks by introducing non-linearity. Without them, the network could only model linear relationships, severely limiting its capabilities. Activation functions like Sigmoid, ReLU (Rectified Linear Unit), and Tanh help the network learn complex patterns. The Sigmoid function, for instance, squashes the input values to a range between 0 and 1, making it useful for binary classification tasks. ReLU is particularly popular in deep learning because it allows faster and more efficient training by activating only the positive input values. Tanh, on the other hand, scales the input values to a range between -1 and 1, making it useful for tasks where the output can take on both positive and negative values.

Neural networks have many practical applications, making them indispensable in various fields. In image and speech recognition, neural networks excel at identifying and categorizing objects, faces and spoken words with remarkable accuracy. For example, your smartphone's facial recognition system uses a neural network to map and identify your face, allowing you to unlock your phone effortlessly. In Natural Language Processing (NLP), neural networks power translation services, enabling seamless communication across different languages. These models analyze and generate human-like text, making it possible for virtual assistants to understand and respond to your queries naturally. Autonomous driving systems also rely heavily on neural networks to interpret real-time data from sensors and cameras, allowing vehicles to navigate roads safely and efficiently.

Understanding neural networks and their real-world applications highlights AI's incredible potential to transform various aspects of our lives. Whether it's making everyday tasks more convenient or advancing technology in fields like healthcare and transportation, neural networks are at the heart of these innovations.

3.3 DEEP LEARNING: BEYOND BASIC MACHINE LEARNING

Deep learning represents a significant leap from traditional machine learning. While machine learning models learn from data to make predictions, deep learning models use neural networks with multiple hidden layers to analyze vast amounts of data and identify intricate patterns. This depth allows them to handle complex tasks with remarkable accuracy. Imagine a traditional machine learning model as a single-level building. In contrast, a deep learning model is like a skyscraper with numerous floors, each adding more detail and sophistication. This architecture enables deep learning models to excel in areas where traditional models might struggle.

Convolutional Neural Networks (CNNs) are a prime example of deep learning's power, especially in image processing. CNNs autonomously extract layered visual representations from image data. They consist of convolutional layers, which apply filters to the input image to create feature maps and pooling layers which reduce the dimensionality of these feature maps while preserving important information. nomously extract layered visual representations from image data. For instance, when you upload a photo to a social media platform and it suggests tags for faces in the image, that's CNN at work. It detects and recognizes objects, people, and even activities within images, making it invaluable for facial recognition systems and object detection tasks. These capabilities have revolutionized fields like security, where facial recognition is crucial, and autonomous vehicles, which rely on image processing to understand and navigate their environment.

Recurrent Neural Networks (RNNs) are another powerful type of deep learning model designed to handle sequential data. Unlike CNNs, which excel at processing static images, RNNs are adept at understanding sequences, such as time series data or natural language. They achieve this by maintaining a form of memory where each output is influenced by the current input and the previous inputs. This makes RNNs particularly effective for tasks like time series prediction, where understanding past trends is crucial for forecasting future values. In language modeling, RNNs can predict the next word in a sentence by considering the context of previous words, enabling applications like text generation and translation. The concept of loops within the network allows RNNs to retain information over time, mimicking the way humans process sequences of data.

Deep learning has also given rise to some of the most advanced AI applications, like Generative Adversarial Networks (GANs). GANs consist of two neural networks, a generator and a discriminator, that work together to create realistic data. The generator produces fake data, while the discriminator evaluates its authenticity. Through this adversarial process, GANs can generate highly realistic images, such as creating lifelike portraits of non-existent people or enhancing low-resolution images to high resolution. Another cutting-edge application is deep reinforcement learning, exemplified by AI systems like AlphaGo. This AI, developed by DeepMind, defeated the world champion in the complex game of Go by learning strategies through millions of simulated games.

Deep reinforcement learning combines deep learning with rein-forcement learning principles, allowing the AI to learn optimal actions through trial and error, significantly advancing the field of gaming AI.

Deep learning's advanced capabilities have also transformed industries beyond gaming and image processing. In healthcare, deep learning models analyze medical images to detect diseases with accuracy comparable to human doctors, providing invaluable support in medical diagnostics. In finance, deep learning models predict stock prices and market trends by analyzing historical data and detecting patterns that traditional models might miss. These applications showcase the versatility and power of deep learning, making it a cornerstone of modern AI advancements.

3.4 REAL-WORLD APPLICATIONS OF MACHINE LEARNING

In healthcare, machine learning is revolutionizing how diseases are diagnosed and treated. Imagine a doctor using an AI-powered tool to analyze medical images to detect conditions like cancer or heart disease. These diagnostic tools sift through millions of data points to identify patterns that even seasoned professionals might miss. Personalized medicine is another groundbreaking applica-tion. By analyzing a patient's genetic information, lifestyle, and medical history, machine-learning models can recommend tailored treatment plans. Predictive analytics also play a crucial role. By evaluating patient data, these models can forecast poten-tial health outcomes, enabling preventive measures and early interventions.

In the financial sector, machine learning is a game-changer for fraud detection and risk management. Picture a bank that uses AI to monitor real-time transactions, flagging suspicious activities that could indicate fraud. These systems learn from past fraudulent patterns to improve their accuracy continually. Machine-learning also excels in the context of algorithmic trading. By analyzing market data, these algorithms execute trades at optimal times, maximizing profits. Risk management benefits from machine learning by assessing credit scores more accurately. By considering a broader range of variables, these models offer a more nuanced view of a person's creditworthiness, reducing the risk for lenders.

Marketing strategies have been transformed by machine learning, making campaigns more targeted and effective. Imagine a company that uses AI to divide its customer base into groups based on purchasing behavior. This segmentation allows for more personalized marketing efforts, increasing engagement and conversion rates. Targeted advertising takes this a step further. Machine learning models analyze user data to deliver ads that are most likely to resonate with each individual. Recommendation systems are another powerful tool. By evaluating past behavior, these systems suggest products that a customer is likely to purchase, enhancing the shopping experience. Customer sentiment analysis is also crucial. By analyzing social media posts and reviews, machine learning can gauge public opinion about a brand, helping companies adjust their strategies accordingly.

Environmental science is another field where machine learning is making significant contributions. Climate modeling, for instance, relies heavily on machine learning to predict future weather patterns and assess the impact of climate change. Models analyze vast amounts of data from sources that include satellite imagery and historical weather records, to make accurate forecasts. Wildlife conservation benefits from machine learning by monitoring animal populations and identifying endangered species. Predictive analytics are used to forecast natural disasters like hurricanes and earthquakes. By analyzing geological and meteorological data, these models can provide early warnings, potentially saving lives and reducing damage.

In healthcare, the transformation extends to administrative tasks as well. Machine learning models streamline operations by automating appointment scheduling, optimizing resource allocation, and managing patient records. Predictive analytics also help hospitals anticipate patient admissions, ensuring that staff and resources are adequately prepared. In finance, portfolio management has seen improvements through machine learning. These models analyze market trends and economic indicators to effectively recommend investment strategies, balancing risk and reward. Marketing departments now use machine learning to predict customer churn, identifying which customers are likely to leave and devising strategies to retain them. Environmental scientists use machine learning for soil analysis, helping farmers optimize crop yields while minimizing environmental impact.

Machine learning's versatility is evident across these diverse applications. It enhances accuracy, improves efficiency, and provides valuable insights that drive better decision-making. Whether it's diagnosing diseases, detecting fraud, targeting ads, or predicting natural disasters, machine learning is at the forefront of technological innovation. Being able to analyze data and identify patterns makes it an indispensable tool in many fields, continually pushing the boundaries of what's possible.

3.5 COMMON ALGORITHMS AND THEIR APPLICATIONS

In the world of machine learning, classification algorithms are pivotal. These algorithms categorize data into predefined classes or groups. Decision trees, for instance, are like flowcharts. This means that each internal node represents a decision based on a feature, and each leaf node represents an outcome. Imagine you're sorting emails into "spam" and "not spam." A decision tree might check for certain keywords and sender addresses to make its decision. Random forests take this further by using multiple decision trees to improve accuracy. Each tree votes on the classification, and the majority decision wins. Support Vector Machines (SVM) are another powerful tool. They find the optimal boundary that separates different classes. In medical diagnosis, SVMs can help classify whether a tumor is benign or malignant by analyzing patient data.

Regression algorithms are crucial for predicting continuous outcomes. Linear regression, one of the simplest forms, models the relationship between a dependent variable and one or more independent variables by using a linear equation. For example, if you're predicting housing prices, linear regression might use features like square footage, number of bedrooms, and location to estimate the price. Polynomial regression is similar but can model non-linear relationships by fitting a polynomial equation to the data. This is useful in scenarios where the relationship between variables is more complex, such as predicting the growth rate of a company based on various financial metrics.

Clustering algorithms group similar data points together, making them invaluable for tasks like customer segmentation. As we have learned, K-means clustering is a popular method where data points are grouped into clusters based on their distance to the cluster's centroid. In retail, K-means can identify groups of customers with similar buying patterns, helping the store tailor its marketing strategies. Hierarchical clustering, another method, builds a hierarchy of clusters. It starts by treating each data point as its own cluster and then merges the closest pairs until only one cluster remains. This approach is useful for anomaly detection, where unusual data points can be identified as separate clusters.

Dimensionality reduction techniques simplify complex datasets by reducing the number of features while maintaining the essential properties. Principal Component Analysis (PCA) is one such technique. It transforms the data into a new coordinate system, where the first few coordinates (principal components) capture the most variance in the data. This makes it easier to visualize high-dimensional data on a 2D or 3D plot. For instance, PCA can help visualize gene expression data, where each gene is a dimension, to identify patterns among different samples. t-Distributed Stochastic Neighbor Embedding (t-SNE) is another technique that excels at visualizing high-dimensional data by mapping it into a lower-dimensional space. It's particularly effective for visualizing clusters in data, making it easier to identify distinct groups.

These algorithms and techniques form the backbone of many machine-learning applications. They help us make sense of vast amounts of data, identify patterns, and make informed decisions. Whether it's classifying emails, predicting market trends, segmenting customers, or visualizing complex datasets, these tools enable us to harness the power of machine learning in practical, impactful ways.

As we conclude this chapter on diving deeper into machine learning, remember that these algorithms are the building blocks of many AI applications. Their ability to analyze data, find patterns, and make predictions is what makes machine learning so powerful.

4

OVERCOMING COMMON OBJECTIONS AND CHALLENGES

L et's face it—we all encounter roadblocks at various times in our lives when it may be easier just to give up rather than persevere. This is where we will address what might hold you back in your AI explorations and hopefully knock those roadblocks over.

You are not alone. Although the idea of exploring AI intrigued me, the thought of having to deal with complex code felt daunting. But that was until I discovered a tool that promised to let me create AI models without writing a single line of code. This discovery was a game-changer that transformed my perception of AI from something intimidating to being accessible and the catalyst that got me on the path to learning more. This chapter is dedicated to those who want to explore AI but feel held back by the mystery of coding and various other challenges.

4.1 AI WITHOUT CODING: SIMPLE PROJECTS FOR BEGINNERS

The concept of no-code AI tools is a recent development that makes AI accessible to everyone, regardless of their technical background. These tools use visual interfaces on top of complex codebases, allowing you to build AI models with drag-and-drop simplicity. Imagine creating an AI model just by arranging blocks on a screen, much like playing with digital LEGO pieces. This approach allows non-programmers to engage with AI in meaningful and fun ways.

One popular no-code AI tool is Google's Teachable Machine. This web-based platform allows you to create image, audio, or pose classification models without writing code. You can upload pictures, record audio clips, or use your webcam to capture different poses, and the tool guides you through the process step-by-step. For instance, you could create an image classifier that distinguishes between cats and dogs by simply uploading a few pictures of each. Another example is training a model to recognize different sounds, such as clapping or snapping fingers, by recording audio samples.

Another powerful platform is Lobe, developed by Microsoft. Lobe enables users to build custom machine learning models without coding. It offers a straightforward interface where you can upload data, label it, and train your model. For example, you could develop a chatbot that understands and responds to basic customer inquiries by providing text examples of questions and answers. The platform's simplicity makes it an excellent choice for beginners who want to experiment with AI without getting bogged down by technical details.

RunwayML is another no-code AI platform designed for creators. It focuses on applications involving images, videos, and text. With RunwayML, you can create AI models using a visual interface, making it ideal for artists, designers, and content creators. Think how rewarding it would be to create a video where the background seamlessly changes based on your movements, or to generate realistic text-based content for your blog. These possibilities are within reach, thanks to RunwayML's user-friendly design.

Let's walk through a simple no-code AI project using Google's Teachable Machine. Suppose you want to create an image classifier. First, go to the Teachable Machine website and choose the image project option. Next, upload images of the categories you would like to classify, such as pictures of cats and dogs. Label each set of images accordingly. Once your images are uploaded and labeled, click the "train" button. The tool will process the images and create a model. Finally, test your model by uploading new images and seeing how accurately it classifies them. This entire process can be completed in minutes, making it an excellent starting point for beginners.

Similarly, with Lobe you can develop a chatbot. Start by opening Lobe and selecting a new project. Upload text samples of common customer questions and provide corresponding answers. Label each question-answer pair. The platform will guide you through training the model. Once trained, test your chatbot by entering new questions and observing the responses. This project introduces you to AI and provides a practical tool you can use.

No-code AI tools come with significant benefits. They make AI accessible to non-programmers, enabling quick prototyping and easy use. It means you can experiment with AI concepts without needing a technical background, perfect for educators, hobbyists and professionals looking to integrate AI into their work.

However, these tools also have limitations in that, as you would expect, they offer less flexibility and customization than coding solutions. Advanced users will most likely find that no-code platforms lack the depth needed for the types of complex projects they are dealing with. Nonetheless, they provide an excellent entry point for anyone interested in AI but not necessarily coding. Although you may find as you progress that you surprise yourself as your curiosity expands.

These tools demystify AI, showing that it's not just for tech experts. You can start with simple projects, gain confidence, and gradually explore more complex aspects of AI. The primary goal of this book is to make AI enjoyable and accessible for everyone.

I highly recommend that you continue exploring, and I have provided resources and guidance to help you with that.

4.2 TIME MANAGEMENT: LEARNING AI ON A BUSY SCHEDULE

Balancing AI learning with a busy life can seem challenging, but with effective time management, it becomes doable. One of the most practical strategies is setting specific achievable goals for each learning session. Instead of vaguely deciding to "study AI," set a clear goal like "complete one lesson on neural networks." This makes your study sessions more focused and productive. Another helpful tip is creating a consistent study schedule that fits into your daily routines. Whether it's dedicating 30 minutes every morning before work or an hour after dinner, consistency helps build a habit, making it easier to stay on track.

Prioritization is key to making the most of your time. Focus on high-impact topics and projects that provide the most value. For instance, if you're interested in machine learning, prioritize foundational topics like supervised and unsupervised learning before getting involved in more complex subjects like deep learning. The Pareto Principle, which suggests that 20% of tasks yield 80% of results, can be a helpful guideline. Identify the critical few tasks that will give you the most significant progress and concentrate your efforts there. This approach ensures that you make substantial advancements even with limited time.

Utilizing tools and resources designed for efficient learning can also make a huge difference. Productivity apps like Trello or Asana help organize tasks, track progress, and set deadlines. These apps allow you to break down your learning objectives into manageable steps and visualize your progress. Learning platforms like Coursera or Udacity offer structured courses with built-in progress tracking and reminders. These platforms often include quizzes and projects that reinforce learning, ensuring you stay engaged and make steady progress.

Making small, consistent efforts is crucial for long-term success. Instead of cramming all your learning into a single lengthy session, break it down into smaller, regular intervals. Even 15 minutes a day can lead to substantial progress over time. This method not only prevents burnout but also helps in retaining information more reliably. Consistency is more important than intensity when it comes to learning complex subjects like AI.

Another effective strategy is integrating learning into your daily routine. Listening to AI podcasts during your commute is a fun way to learn, read articles during lunch breaks, or watch tutorial videos while dinner cooks. This way, you're continuously exposed to new information without needing to carve out large blocks of time. Additionally, using flashcards or apps like Anki for spaced repetition can help reinforce key concepts and terminologies, making them easier to recall.

Don't underestimate the importance of taking breaks and rewarding yourself. Set milestones and celebrate when you reach them, whether it's finishing a challenging course or successfully completing a project. These small rewards can keep you motivated and make the learning process more enjoyable. Engaging with others who share your interests by joining study groups or online communities can provide support, offer different perspectives and keep you coming back for more.

Find a balance between work, personal life and learning. Tell your family and friends about your goals so that you can set boundaries and create a peaceful and productive learning environment. Remember, it's okay to adjust your schedule and goals as needed. Flexibility allows you to adapt to unexpected changes without feeling overwhelmed. These strategies ensure you make meaningful progress without sacrificing other important aspects of your life, and by making consistent efforts, you can integrate AI learning into your busy schedule.

4.3 MATH ANXIETY: UNDERSTANDING AI WITHOUT ADVANCED MATHEMATICS

It's common to feel anxious about the math involved in AI, and you might think pursuing an interest in AI requires a deep understanding of complex mathematical concepts. If this is you, the good news is that many AI projects don't demand advanced math knowledge. Many AI tools and platforms handle the underlying math for you, so you can focus on applications like Google's Teachable Machine or Microsoft's Lobe, which abstract the complexities, allowing you to build and train models without needing to understand every mathematical detail behind them. This means you can create impactful AI solutions with a basic understanding of the concepts.

A fundamental grasp of key mathematical ideas is often enough for beginner projects. Resources like Khan Academy offer excellent courses that simplify linear algebra and calculus, making these subjects accessible to everyone. These courses break down complex topics into manageable lessons, using clear explanations and practical examples. Another great resource is the YouTube channel 3Blue1Brown, which visualizes math concepts in a way that makes them easier to understand. Watching these videos can help demystify the math behind AI, offering intuitive explanations that resonate with learners of all backgrounds.

Step-by-step guides for performing basic mathematical operations used in AI can also be incredibly helpful. Let's take the example of calculating the mean and standard deviation of a dataset. Begin by listing all the values in your dataset. Next, add them together and divide by the number of values to find the mean. To calculate the standard deviation, subtract the mean from each value, square the result, and find the average of these squared differences. Finally, take the square root of this average. By breaking down these operations into clear, manageable steps, you can build confidence in handling the math involved in AI projects.

Another approach is to use software tools that perform these calculations for you. For instance, Python libraries like NumPy and Pandas offer functions that simplify statistical computations. If you want to calculate the mean of a dataset using Python, you can use the numpy.mean() function. Similarly, the pandas.DataFrame.std() function calculates the standard deviation of data in a DataFrame. These tools allow you to focus on interpreting the results rather than getting bogged down by the calculations themselves.

You can overcome math anxiety and confidently engage with AI by simplifying key concepts and leveraging resources that break down complex topics. The focus shifts from mastering the math to understanding how to apply these concepts effectively in your projects. This approach makes AI accessible to everyone, regardless of their mathematical background.

4.4 FINDING RELIABLE RESOURCES: SEPARATING FACT FROM FICTION

Regarding resources, the trick is not to let yourself get overwhelmed by the sheer volume of online information about AI. Not all sources were created equal, and just using reliable ones and knowing how to identify them is crucial for building a solid and reliable foundation of knowledge. Accurate information helps you avoid the pitfalls of misinformation and outdated practices, ensuring you learn the most current and effective techniques. Reliable resources provide clarity and depth, allowing you to make informed decisions and progress confidently in your AI journey.

Evaluating the credibility of resources requires a few steps. For example, platforms like Goodreads for books or course review sections on educational websites can offer valuable insights into the resource's quality and effectiveness. Peer reviews often highlight both strengths and weaknesses, helping you make an informed choice.

Several reputable AI learning platforms stand out for their high-quality education. Coursera offers excellent courses from top universities and institutions, providing both theoretical and practical knowledge and courses like "Machine Learning" by Andrew Ng which have become foundational for many AI learners. edX provides professional certificates and degrees from renowned universities, offering structured and accredited programs. Fast.ai focuses on practical AI courses with a hands-on approach, making complex topics accessible and engaging. These platforms are trusted sources that ensure you receive a comprehensive and accurate education in AI.

When I started exploring AI, I came across several resources that promised quick and easy mastery of the subject. It didn't take long to realize that these claims were too good to be true. They scratched the surface and failed to provide a deeper understanding of the fundamental concepts. This taught me the importance of using reliable resources, and ones that dig a little deeper than complete basics. Trustworthy sources lay the groundwork for meaningful learning, whereas unreliable ones can lead to confusion and frustration. By focusing on reputable platforms, you can build a strong foundation in AI and avoid the common pitfalls of misinformation.

4.5 STAYING MOTIVATED: TIPS FOR SELF-PACED LEARNING

Self-paced learning comes with its own set of challenges. We have looked at time management, goals and prioritization, but you can still do more to help yourself stay focused.

Making the learning process enjoyable and rewarding really helps. Incorporate gamified learning platforms that offer challenges and rewards to make studying more engaging. Platforms like Duolingo and Codecademy use gamification to keep users motivated by turning learning into a game. Exploring creative AI projects that align with your personal interests can also make the process more satisfying. If you love photography, for example, consider working on an AI project that involves image recognition or enhancement. By connecting your learning to your passions, you make it more relevant and enjoyable.

Another strategy is to diversify your learning methods. Mix up your routine by incorporating different types of content, such as videos, podcasts, articles, and interactive tutorials. This variety can keep things interesting and prevent burnout. Setting up a dedicated learning space can help you stay focused. A quiet, organized, and comfortable environment can make a significant difference in your ability to concentrate and stay motivated.

Above all, stay consistent. Remember, even small, regular efforts can lead to substantial progress over time. Stick to the time you have dedicated to your AI studies as much as possible. Track your progress regularly by keeping a journal or using an app to record what you've learned and achieved. This is a great way to provide a sense of accomplishment and help you see how far you've come.

Lastly, don't hesitate to seek inspiration from others. Reading success stories of individuals who have mastered AI or achieved significant milestones can be incredibly motivating. These stories can provide insights into effective strategies and remind you that your goals are attainable. Surround yourself with positive influences to encourage you on your learning path, and perhaps soon, you can find yourself inspiring others.

MAKE A DIFFERENCE

UNLOCK THE POWER OF GENEROSITY

"The best way to find yourself is to lose yourself in the service of others."

— MAHATMA GANDHI

Helping others brings joy and makes the world a better place. Now, you can help someone who's curious about Artificial Intelligence but unsure where to begin!

My mission with *The Essentials of AI for Beginners: A Step-by-step Guide to Grasp AI Concepts, Stay Current with Future Trends, and Uncover Practical Applications* is to make AI simple, accessible and fun for everyone.

To reach more people, I need your help!

People often pick books based on reviews. By leaving a review, you can guide someone just like you—someone starting out in AI—on their learning journey. Your review could help…

- a small business owner understand AI to grow their business
- an entrepreneur use AI to support their family
- an employee gain new skills to excel in their career
- a reader unlock the power of AI and transform their life.

It only takes a minute, and it's free, but your review could change someone's path in understanding AI and even transform their life.

To make a difference, simply scan the QR code below and leave your review:

Together, we can spread knowledge and help others embrace the future!

With heart-felt gratitude

Caroline Hylands

5

BALANCING THEORY AND PRACTICAL APPLICATION

I magine you're building a complex LEGO structure. You have all the pieces but without understanding the instructions, your creation might not come together as intended. This chapter is about providing you with the theoretical foundations of AI, much like those LEGO instructions. Understanding these concepts will help you construct AI models that are not only effective but also insightful.

5.1 THEORETICAL FOUNDATIONS OF AI: KEY CONCEPTS

The concept of intelligence and how it's simulated lies at the core of AI. Intelligence in humans encompasses learning, reasoning, problem-solving and adapting. AI aims to replicate these abilities in machines. One fundamental theory that underpins AI is the idea of Turing machines and the Turing Test. Proposed by Alan Turing, a Turing machine is a mathematical model that manipulates symbols on a strip of tape according to a set of rules. It serves as a basic model of computation. The Turing Test on the other hand, assesses a machine's ability to exhibit human-like intelligence. If a human interrogator cannot reliably distinguish the machine from another human based on its responses, the machine is said to pass the test.

In the early days of AI, two primary approaches emerged: symbolic AI and connectionist AI. Symbolic AI, also known as "good old-fashioned AI" (GOFAI), relies on explicit rules and symbols to represent knowledge. Think of it as using a detailed recipe to bake a cake. Connectionist AI, in contrast, uses neural networks that mimic the human brain's structure and function. This approach focuses on learning from data rather than following predefined rules. It's like teaching someone to bake by letting them experiment and learn from their mistakes.

Mathematics plays a vital role in AI, providing the tools and frameworks necessary for developing and understanding AI models. Probability theory is one such mathematical foundation. It deals with the likelihood of events occurring and helps model uncertainties. For instance, in spam detection, probability theory helps figure out the likelihood that an email is spam based on its features. Probability distributions, random variables and expected values are key concepts in probability theory that are essential for various machine learning algorithms.

Linear algebra is another cornerstone of AI, particularly in understanding neural networks. Concepts like vectors, matrices and matrix multiplication are fundamental in representing and manipulating data. When training a neural network, linear algebra helps perform operations on data efficiently, enabling the model to learn from large datasets. Calculus, especially in optimization, is crucial for fine-tuning AI models. Gradient descent, an optimization algorithm, uses calculus to minimize the error in a model by adjusting its parameters. This reiterative process ensures that the model becomes more accurate over time.

While these mathematical principles are important, it's reassuring to know that advanced math is not always necessary for AI projects. Many AI tools and platforms abstract the underlying math, allowing you to focus on application rather than complex equations. For example, platforms like TensorFlow and PyTorch handle the heavy lifting of mathematical computations, enabling you to build and train models with minimal mathematical intervention. Basic understanding of concepts is often sufficient for beginner projects, making AI accessible to those without a strong math background.

Machine learning theories provide deeper insights into building effective models. One crucial concept is the bias-variance tradeoff. This tradeoff involves balancing a model's ability to generalize to new data (bias) and its sensitivity to fluctuations in the training data (variance). A model with high bias oversimplifies the data, leading to underfitting. Conversely, a model with high variance overfits the data, capturing noise along with the signal. Regularization techniques such as L1 and L2 regularization, help mitigate overfitting by adding a penalty to the model's complexity, ensuring it generalizes better to new data.

Theoretical knowledge significantly informs practical AI work. For instance, understanding the bias-variance tradeoff helps improve model accuracy by guiding the selection and tuning of algorithms. Theory also aids in troubleshooting and refining AI models. When a model underperforms, theoretical insights can identify whether the issue lies in the data, the algorithm, or the model's complexity. Mathematical principles are essential in feature engineering, the process of selecting and transforming variables to improve model performance. By applying these principles, you can create more effective models that yield valuable insights.

5.2 PRACTICAL AI: APPLYING THEORY TO REAL-WORLD PROBLEMS

Translating theoretical knowledge into practical AI applications begins with identifying the right techniques for specific problems. Consider a company looking to optimize its supply chain logistics. The theoretical concepts of predictive modeling and optimization algorithms come into play here. By analyzing historical data on inventory levels, shipping times and demand patterns, predictive models can forecast future needs, allowing the company to adjust its logistics operations proactively. This application of theory to practice involves mapping these theoretical models to actionable steps, such as adjusting reorder points or selecting optimal shipping routes.

Another practical application is enhancing customer service using AI-driven chatbots. The theoretical foundations of Natural Language Processing (NLP) and machine learning guide the development of these chatbots. Understanding customer queries and providing accurate responses requires training models on vast datasets of conversational text. By applying these theoretical insights, businesses can develop chatbots that not only understand and respond to common customer inquiries but also improve over time through machine learning. This involves choosing the right algorithms, and then training the models, whilst continuously refining them based on user interactions.

Personalizing marketing strategies with recommendation systems is another area where theory meets practice. Companies like

Netflix use collaborative filtering and content-based filtering to recommend shows and movies to their users. These recommendation systems rely on theoretical concepts such as matrix factorization and similarity measures and by analyzing user behavior and preferences, these systems can suggest content that aligns with individual tastes, enhancing user engagement and satisfaction. The practical implementation involves collecting and processing user data, training the recommendation algorithms, and integrating them into the user interface for seamless personalization.

Domain expertise plays a crucial role in applying AI theory to practical problems. Collaborating with industry experts helps bridge the gap between theoretical models and real-world applications. For instance, in healthcare, AI developers work closely with medical professionals to understand the nuances of diagnosing diseases. This collaboration ensures that AI models are tailored to fit the specific needs of the industry. Similarly, in finance, AI solutions are adapted to meet regulatory requirements and financial norms, thanks to the input of financial experts.

Successful cross-disciplinary projects highlight the importance of combining AI theory with domain-specific knowledge. In agriculture, AI models have been developed to predict crop yields and optimize irrigation schedules. These models are informed by agricultural science, ensuring they address the unique challenges of farming. In the energy sector, AI is used to predict equipment failures and optimize maintenance schedules, blending the expertise of engineers with predictive modeling techniques. These examples demonstrate how domain knowledge enhances the relevance and effectiveness of AI applications.

To effectively apply AI theory, consider iterative development and continuous learning. Start with a basic model and gradually refine it through multiple iterations. This approach allows you to incorporate feedback and improve the model's performance over time. Validation and testing are also crucial in practical applications. Regularly evaluate your models against real-world data to ensure they remain accurate and reliable. Leverage existing frameworks and libraries to streamline development. Tools like TensorFlow, PyTorch, and Scikit-learn provide pre-built functions and algorithms that will save time and effort. By using these resources, you can focus on fine-tuning your models rather than building everything from scratch.

In the practical implementation of AI, understanding the problem context, selecting the right techniques, and continuously refining your models are key to success. Combining theoretical insights with practical steps enables you to develop AI solutions that are both effective and relevant to real-world challenges.

5.3 CASE STUDIES IN AI: LEARNING FROM SUCCESSES AND FAILURES

Studying case studies in AI is like peeking behind the curtain of a grand stage production. You see not just the polished performance but also the behind-the-scenes efforts, mistakes and adjustments that make it all work. Real-world implementations offer invaluable lessons. By analyzing both successes and failures, you can understand common pitfalls and best practices and gain insights into the iterative nature of AI projects. This approach helps you navigate your AI endeavors more effectively, armed with the wisdom of those who have walked this path before.

One notable success story is Netflix's recommendation engine, with which users find content they enjoy more quickly, leading to longer viewing times and higher satisfaction. The recommendation engine saves Netflix over a billion dollars annually by reducing churn rates and increasing customer loyalty. A win-win I'd say.

IBM Watson's success in healthcare diagnostics is another compelling example. Watson uses natural language processing and machine learning to analyze vast amounts of medical data. It assists doctors in diagnosing diseases, recommending treatments and even predicting patient outcomes. By processing medical literature, patient records, and clinical trial data, Watson provides evidence-based insights that enhance decision-making. This AI application has demonstrated remarkable accuracy in diagnosing conditions like cancer, often identifying patterns that human doctors might miss. The success of IBM Watson showcases the transformative potential of AI in improving healthcare outcomes and reducing diagnostic errors.

Google's self-driving car project represents a monumental technological advancement in the field of autonomous vehicles. The project combines computer vision, machine learning, and sensor fusion to navigate roads, avoid obstacles, and make real-time driving decisions. Since 2020, Google's self-driving cars have logged millions of miles, demonstrating the feasibility and safety of autonomous driving. This project highlights the iterative nature of AI development, with continuous refinements and updates based on real-world testing. The success of this project paves the way for a future where autonomous vehicles could reduce traffic accidents, improve mobility, and transform transportation systems.

However, not all AI projects have smooth sailing. Microsoft's Tay chatbot, released in 2016, is a cautionary tale. Designed to chat with users on social media, Tay was an experiment in unsupervised learning. Within hours, users manipulated Tay into generating inappropriate and offensive content, forcing Microsoft to take it offline. This incident illustrates the challenges of deploying AI in uncontrolled environments, highlighting the importance of robust content moderation, ethical considerations and contingency plans for AI projects interacting with the public.

The failure to predict the 2008 financial crisis is another example. Many AI models used in finance failed to foresee the collapse due to their reliance on historical data that did not account for the unprecedented conditions. This failure emphasizes the limitations of AI models when faced with black swan events—rare and unpredictable occurrences. It also underscores the need for incorporating diverse data sources and stress-testing models against extreme scenarios to enhance their robustness and reliability.

AI systems in legal and ethical contexts face their own set of challenges. For instance, predictive policing algorithms have been criticized for perpetuating biases present in historical crime data. These biases can lead to unfair targeting of certain communities, raising ethical concerns about the use of AI in law enforcement. This highlights the critical need for transparency, accountability, and fairness in AI development and deployment. Ensuring that AI systems are free from bias and do not reinforce existing inequalities is paramount for their ethical use.

From these case studies, several key lessons emerge. The quality and representativeness of data are crucial for building effective AI models. Comprehensive testing and validation are necessary to ensure models perform well in real-world conditions. Ethical considerations must be integral to AI development, ensuring that systems are fair, transparent and accountable. By learning from both the triumphs and setbacks of these projects you can navigate the complex landscape of AI with greater confidence.

5.4 AI EXPERIMENTATION: TESTING AND ITERATING

Experimentation is the backbone of AI development. At its core, it mirrors the scientific method. You start with a hypothesis, test it, and iterate based on the results. This cycle of hypothesis, testing, and iteration is crucial for refining AI models and ensuring they perform well. For instance, if you're developing a model to predict customer churn, your initial hypothesis might be that transaction frequency is a key predictor. You test this by training a model with this feature and then evaluating its performance. Based on the results, you might adjust your hypothesis, perhaps considering customer feedback scores as another important factor.

Effective AI experimentation requires strategic approaches. One such method is A/B testing. In this process, you compare two versions of a model to see which performs better. For example, you might test two different algorithms for predicting sales, each trained on the same dataset but using different features or techniques. A/B testing helps you identify the most effective approach by directly comparing their performance. Cross-validation is another powerful technique. It involves splitting your data into multiple subsets, training and validating the model on different combinations of these subsets. This provides a robust evaluation of the model's performance, ensuring it generalizes well to new data. Hyperparameter tuning takes this a step further by optimizing the model's parameters. Imagine you're fine-tuning the engine of a race car; hyperparameter tuning adjusts the settings to maximize performance.

Practical examples of AI experimentation abound. Experimenting with different neural network architectures can lead to significant improvements. You might start with a simple feedforward network and then experiment with adding more layers or using different activation functions. Testing various data preprocessing techniques is another area ripe for experimentation. For instance, you could compare the performance of a model trained on raw data versus one trained on normalized data. Iterating on feature selection and engineering also plays a crucial role. By experimenting with different sets of features, you can identify which ones contribute most to the model's accuracy. Each experiment provides insights that help refine and improve the model.

Several tools and platforms facilitate AI experimentation. Jupyter Notebooks are invaluable for interactive experimentation. They allow you to write and run code in cells, making it easy to test different approaches and visualize results in real time. Leveraging cloud platforms like AWS or Google Cloud enables scalable testing. These platforms provide the computational power needed to train and test models on large datasets, allowing you to run multiple experiments in parallel. Tools like TensorBoard are also essential. TensorBoard visualizes experiment results, showing how different model configurations impact performance. This helps you make informed decisions about which changes to pursue further.

Experimentation in AI is not just about trial and error; it's a structured process that drives innovation and improvement. By systematically testing different approaches and learning from the results, you can develop AI models that are both effective and reliable. Whether you're adjusting the architecture of a neural network, fine-tuning hyperparameters, or exploring new data preprocessing techniques, each experiment brings you closer to a model that meets your goals.

5.5 BRIDGING THE GAP: FROM THEORY TO PRACTICE

Transitioning from theoretical AI knowledge to practical application presents several challenges. One major hurdle is the complexity of real-world data compared to theoretical models. In theory, data is often clean, well-structured and free of noise. However, real-world data is messy, incomplete and full of inconsistencies. Handling this requires sound data preprocessing techniques and a keen eye for identifying anomalies. Another challenge is managing the trade-off between model performance and interpretability. Complex models like deep neural networks may deliver excellent performance but are often black boxes, making it difficult to understand their decision-making processes. Balancing accuracy with transparency is crucial, especially in fields like healthcare and finance where decisions have significant consequences.

Scalability is another concern when moving theoretical models to production environments. A model that works well on a small dataset might struggle with large-scale data due to computational limitations. Ensuring that your model can handle increased data volume and complexity without compromising performance is essential. This involves optimizing algorithms, using efficient data structures, and leveraging parallel processing capabilities. Addressing these challenges requires a thoughtful approach, blending theoretical insights with practical strategies.

Several strategies can help bridge the gap between theory and practice effectively. Start with simple models and iterate towards complexity. Begin with a basic linear regression model before moving on to more complex algorithms like random forests or neural networks. This iterative approach allows you to build a solid foundation and gradually refine your model. Prototyping and pilot projects are invaluable for validating approaches. Develop a small-scale prototype to test your model's feasibility and effectiveness. Use this as a learning opportunity to identify potential issues and areas for improvement before scaling up.

Collaboration with cross-functional teams enhances the transition process. Work with data engineers, domain experts and business stakeholders to ensure your model aligns with organizational goals and addresses real-world problems. For instance, collaborating with healthcare professionals can provide insights into clinical workflows, helping you tailor your AI solution to fit the specific needs of medical practitioners. Comprehensive solutions emerge from such collaborations, integrating theoretical knowledge with practical expertise.

Successful transitions from theory to practice offer valuable lessons. Take the example of a machine learning model developed for a recommendation system. Initially, the model might perform well in a controlled environment but falter when exposed to real-world user interactions. By iterating on the model, incorporating user feedback, and refining algorithms, the system can evolve into a robust recommendation engine that enhances user experience and boosts engagement. Another example is a predictive maintenance model implemented in manufacturing. The model predicts equipment failures, allowing for timely maintenance and reducing downtime. This transition involves continuous monitoring and updating of the model based on operational data, ensuring sustained performance and reliability.

Continuous feedback and learning are crucial for ongoing success. Establish monitoring systems to track the performance of live AI models. This helps identify issues early and make necessary adjustments. Feedback loops play an essential role in refining and enhancing models. Collect feedback from end-users, analyze performance metrics and use these insights to improve your model. Adapting models to changing real-world conditions is also essential. As new data becomes available or user needs evolve, update your model to maintain its relevance and effectiveness.

In summary, bridging the gap between theory and practice in AI involves overcoming data complexity, balancing performance with interpretability and ensuring scalability. Effective strategies include starting simple, using prototypes and collaborating with diverse teams. Successful transitions demonstrate the importance of continuous feedback and adaptation, leading to practical AI solutions.

6

CAREER ADVANCEMENT WITH AI

You're standing at a crossroads, a place where technology meets career aspirations. You've heard about AI transforming industries, reshaping job roles and creating new opportunities. But how can you navigate this intersection to advance your own career? This chapter is your map, guiding you through the various AI-related roles and the skills you need to thrive in them.

6.1 AI IN TECH CAREERS: ROLES AND RESPONSIBILITIES

In the tech world, AI has carved out many roles, each with its unique responsibilities and opportunities for growth, so let's explore some of these key roles. A Data Scientist, for instance, is like a modern-day detective, sifting through vast amounts of data to uncover patterns and insights. Your day might involve cleaning and preprocessing data to make it usable, then developing models to analyze it, such as working on a project to predict customer behavior based on past purchases and helping businesses make informed decisions.

Next, consider the role of a Machine Learning Engineer. This position focuses more on designing and implementing machine learning models. You're the architect and builder, creating systems that learn and improve from experience. One day, you might train a model to recognize speech patterns; the next, you're optimizing it for better performance. It's a role that requires a complete understanding of algorithms and the ability to fine-tune models to achieve the best results.

Then there's the AI Research Scientist, an explorer pushing the boundaries of what's possible with AI. Your work involves conducting advanced research to develop new algorithms and models. This could mean publishing research papers, collaborating with academic institutions, or even presenting your findings at conferences. How exciting would it be to discover a new method for natural language processing that could revolutionize how virtual assistants understand and interact with users? It's a role that combines creativity with rigorous scientific inquiry.

To excel in these roles, certain skills and qualifications are essential. Proficiency in programming languages like Python and R is a must. These languages are the backbone of AI development, enabling you to write the code that powers machine learning models. Understanding machine learning frameworks such as TensorFlow and PyTorch is equally important. These frameworks provide the tools needed to build and train complex models efficiently. A strong foundation in mathematics and statistics is also crucial. Concepts like linear algebra, calculus, and probability form the basis of machine learning algorithms, helping you understand how models work and how to improve them.

So what would the day-to-day responsibilities of these roles be? As a Data Scientist, your tasks might include data cleaning—removing errors and inconsistencies to ensure the data is accurate and reliable. You'll develop data models to analyze trends and make predictions, often using visualization tools to present your findings in a clear and compelling way. Machine Learning Engineers, on the other hand, spend their days training and deploying ML models. This involves building the models and continuously optimizing them to improve performance. You might use techniques like hyperparameter tuning to fine-tune the model's settings, ensuring it delivers the best possible results.

AI Research Scientists have a different focus. Their day might start with reviewing the latest research in AI, identifying gaps, and brainstorming new ideas. They conduct experiments, often using large datasets to test their hypotheses. Collaboration is key, as they work with other researchers and institutions to validate their findings. Publishing research papers and presenting at conferences are also integral parts of the job, contributing to the broader AI community and advancing the field.

Career advancement in AI tech roles is promising and varied. You can move from junior to senior positions, gaining more responsibility and autonomy over your projects. Another path is transitioning to leadership roles, such as an AI Team Leader or even a Chief AI Officer. These positions involve overseeing AI strategies and guiding teams to achieve organizational goals. Specialization is yet another avenue. You could focus on Natural Language Processing (NLP), diving deep into how machines understand and generate human language. Alternatively, specializing in computer vision could see you working on projects that enable machines to interpret visual data, such as facial recognition systems or autonomous vehicles.

As you navigate these roles and responsibilities, remember that the field of AI is dynamic and continually evolving. Staying updated with the latest advancements and continuously honing your skills will enhance your career prospects and keep you at the forefront of this exciting field.

6.2 NON-TECH CAREERS: ENHANCING YOUR ROLE WITH AI

Suppose you're a marketing manager for a mid-sized company. You've always relied on traditional methods for customer segmentation, like basic demographic data and purchase history. Now, with AI, you can use predictive analytics to dive deeper. By analyzing patterns in customer behavior, AI can help you identify segments you might have missed. For example, it can reveal that certain customers prefer to shop during specific times of the year, allowing you to tailor your advertising campaigns more effectively. This level of insight can transform your marketing strategies, making them more targeted and efficient.

In healthcare, AI is a game-changer. As a healthcare professional, you could use an AI tool that analyzes patient data to provide an early diagnosis and personalized treatment plans. This in turn improves patient outcomes and streamlines your workflow.

Education is another field where AI can make a significant impact. As a teacher, you're always looking for ways to personalize learning experiences for your students. AI-driven platforms can analyze each student's learning style, strengths, and weaknesses and then tailor lesson plans accordingly. For instance, if a student struggles with mathematics, the AI can recommend specific exercises and resources to help them improve. This customized approach not only enhances the learning experience but also helps students achieve better academic outcomes.

To enhance your skills with AI, start by learning basic AI concepts and tools relevant to your field. You don't need a deep technical background to get started. Begin with online courses that cover the fundamentals of AI and machine learning. Platforms like Coursera and Udacity offer courses specifically designed for non-tech professionals. These courses often include practical examples and hands-on projects which mean you can apply what you've learned in real-world scenarios. Attending workshops and conferences can also be beneficial. These events provide opportunities to learn from experts, network with peers, and keep up to date on the latest trends and advancements in AI.

Consider the example of a marketing manager who successfully integrated AI into their role. By using AI tools for targeted advertising campaigns, they were able to reach the most relevant target group, resulting in higher engagement and conversion rates. This success boosted their company's revenue and positioned them as a forward-thinking leader in their industry. Similarly, a teacher utilizing AI-driven platforms to tailor lesson plans saw significant improvements in student performance and engagement. The AI provided insights into each student's progress, enabling the teacher to offer more personalized support and resources.

To support your professional development, numerous resources are available. Online courses like Coursera and Udacity offer comprehensive AI training tailored to various fields. Industry-specific workshops and conferences provide opportunities for hands-on learning and networking. AI-focused communities and forums, such as AI4ALL, offer a platform to engage with other professionals, share knowledge, and stay updated on developments. These resources help you create a strong foundation in AI, enhancing your skills and opening up new opportunities in your career.

6.3 FREELANCING WITH AI SKILLS: OPPORTUNITIES AND PLATFORMS

Freelancing with AI skills opens up a world of flexible and diverse opportunities. For example, by working on data analysis and visualization projects for various clients, you could be helping a small business understand its customer demographics or assisting a healthcare provider in visualizing patient data trends. An advantage you have as a freelancer is focusing on projects that align with your interests and expertise. Developing custom machine learning models for clients is another exciting avenue. From creating predictive models for e-commerce platforms to designing algorithms for financial forecasting, the possibilities are vast. AI consultancy services are also in high demand. Companies often need expert advice on how to implement AI solutions effectively. As a consultant, you could guide businesses through the complexities of AI, from selecting the right tools to optimizing existing systems.

Popular freelancing platforms offer a variety of opportunities for AI professionals. Upwork is a prominent freelance marketplace where you can find numerous AI projects. Here, clients post detailed job descriptions, and you can bid on the ones that best match your skills. Freelancer is another platform that features job postings for AI-related tasks. It allows you to showcase your portfolio and connect with potential clients. Toptal stands out by connecting top AI freelancers with companies looking for specialized expertise. This platform is known for its rigorous vetting process, ensuring that only the best freelancers make it through. This can be particularly advantageous if you're looking to work on high-profile projects with reputable clients.

Building a strong freelance profile is crucial for attracting clients and securing projects. Highlighting relevant AI projects and skills in your profile can make a significant difference. Include detailed descriptions of past projects, emphasizing the impact and results you achieved. Obtaining certifications from recognized institutions can also enhance your credibility. Coursera and Udacity offer certifications in various AI disciplines, which you can showcase in your profile. Collecting client testimonials and building a portfolio of your work can further strengthen your profile. Positive feedback from happy clients builds trust and demonstrate your reliability and expertise.

Managing freelance projects effectively requires clear communication and organization. Start by setting clear project goals and timelines with your clients. This helps ensure that there is a mutual understanding of the project scope and deliverables. Regular updates and open communication channels can prevent misunderstandings and keep the project on track. When discussing project details, being specific about your needs and expectations will help avoid potential issues and ensure smoother collaboration. Needless to say, delivering high-quality work is essential for building a good reputation and securing repeat business, and consistently meeting or exceeding client expectations will lead to long-term relationships and more opportunities.

Freelancing with AI skills offers a unique blend of flexibility and challenge. You can choose projects that align with your interests and expertise while working on diverse tasks. The key to success lies in building a strong profile, effectively managing projects, and continuously expanding your skill set. As you gain experience and build a solid reputation, the opportunities for growth and advancement will only increase.

6.4 AI FOR ENTREPRENEURS: INNOVATING YOUR BUSINESS

Online shopping has become a regular part of everyday life. What if the next step was being greeted by an AI-powered customer service solution? This virtual assistant would answer your questions, guide you through your purchase, and even suggest products based on your preferences. AI-driven customer service solutions are transforming how businesses interact with their customers. They provide instant, personalized responses, enhancing customer satisfaction and minimizing human involvement in routine inquiries. Implementing such solutions can save time, reduce operational costs, and provide a seamless customer experience.

Personalized e-commerce recommendations are a powerful AI-driven business idea. The online retail platform uses AI to analyze your browsing history, purchase patterns, and preferences to suggest products you might like. This personalization goes beyond simple product recommendations, though. It can tailor the entire shopping experience. For instance, the homepage can be customized to display products that align with your interests. In this way, businesses can leverage AI to increase sales, improve customer retention, and enhance the overall shopping experience.

Predictive maintenance services for industrial equipment are revolutionizing the manufacturing sector. Imagine a factory where AI monitors machinery in real time, predicting when maintenance is needed before a breakdown actually happens. This proactive approach prevents costly downtime and extends the lifespan of equipment. AI analyzes data from sensors on the machines, identifying patterns that indicate potential issues. This data-driven approach ensures maintenance is performed only when necessary, optimizing resources and reducing costs. Implementing predictive maintenance can significantly improve operational efficiency and reliability.

Existing businesses can integrate AI to improve operations in various ways. Automating routine tasks is a straightforward yet impactful implementation. Imagine a business where mundane tasks like data entry, scheduling, and inventory management are handled by AI. This allows employees to focus on more strategic activities, increasing overall productivity. AI can also enhance data-driven decision-making. By analyzing large datasets, AI can uncover insights that inform business strategies, from marketing campaigns to product development. These analytics provide a deeper understanding of market trends, customer behavior, and operational efficiencies.

Enhancing customer experiences with AI chatbots is another practical application. Picture a customer visiting your website and interacting with a chatbot that can provide instant support, answer queries, and even process orders. AI chatbots are available 24/7, ensuring customers receive timely assistance. They can handle multiple interactions simultaneously, reducing delay and improving customer satisfaction. Businesses can use AI chatbots to provide a consistent, high-quality customer experience while reducing the workload on human support staff.

For AI startups, funding and resources are crucial. Venture capital and angel investors focused on AI provide financial backing and strategic support, and these investors are often looking for innovative solutions with high growth potential. Government grants and innovation programs are also valuable resources. Many governments offer funding and support for AI research and development, encouraging innovation in the tech sector. AI incubators and accelerators provide mentorship, resources, and networking opportunities to help startups grow. These programs often include access to industry experts, potential investors and collaborative opportunities with other startups.

Successful AI startups offer valuable lessons and inspiration. Consider a startup that uses an AI-driven platform for real-time language translation. This platform enables seamless communication across different languages, breaking down barriers in global interactions. Another success story is a company offering AI-powered cybersecurity solutions. Their AI continuously monitors network traffic, detecting and responding to threats in real time, ensuring reliable protection against cyber-attacks.

6.5 SUCCESS STORIES: CAREER TRANSFORMATIONS WITH AI

Meet Sarah, a data analyst who once spent her days combing through spreadsheets and generating reports. Her work involved interpreting complex datasets, but she always felt there was more she could do. Intrigued by the potential of AI, she decided to investigate further. She began by taking online courses in machine learning and AI, dedicating her evenings and weekends to study. The transition wasn't easy and balancing her job while learning new technical skills was demanding. But Sarah was determined. She started small, applying machine learning models to her existing data projects. Gradually, her skills improved, and so did her confidence. Today Sarah is an AI Research Scientist. She conducts advanced research, develops new algorithms, and collaborates with academic institutions. Her journey from data analyst to AI researcher is a testament to the power of continuous learning and adaptation.

Now let's talk about John, a marketing professional who saw the writing on the wall. The marketing landscape was changing rapidly, and AI was at the forefront of this transformation. John decided to embrace this change rather than resist it. He started by learning the basics of AI and machine learning, focusing on how they could enhance marketing strategies. John faced numerous challenges, including staying updated with AI advancements and balancing his job responsibilities with his new learning goals. However, he persisted. He began using AI tools for targeted advertising campaigns, analyzing customer data to create more effective marketing strategies. Over time, John transitioned into an AI consultant role, advising other companies on leveraging AI for their marketing efforts. His ability to adapt and integrate AI into his work opened new career opportunities and positioned him as a leader in his field.

Both Sarah and John faced considerable obstacles. Learning new technical skills required significant time investment, and keeping abreast with the rapid advancements in AI was challenging. Balancing their existing job responsibilities while acquiring new skills was another hurdle. However, they overcame these challenges through dedication and persistence. They set clear career goals and planned steps to achieve them. They sought mentorship and guidance from experienced professionals, leveraging their networks for support and opportunities. Their journeys highlight the benefits of continuous learning and adaptation in the ever-evolving field of AI.

Key takeaways from Sarah and John's experiences include the necessity of setting clear career goals. Being clear about what you want to achieve helps plan the steps needed to get there. Seeking mentorship is another crucial element. Experienced professionals can provide valuable guidance, helping you navigate the complexities of AI. Leveraging professional networks for support and opportunities can also make a significant difference. Whether it's finding the right course, getting advice on a project, or connecting with potential employers, a strong network is invaluable. Finally, staying persistent and resilient is essential. The path to integrating AI into your career is not always smooth, but those who stay the course and adapt to challenges often find success.

For aspiring AI professionals, actionable advice starts with setting clear career goals. Be clear about what you want to achieve and break it down into manageable steps. Find mentors who can guide you and provide insights based on their experiences. Stay persistent, even when faced with challenges. The field of AI is dynamic and constantly evolving, requiring continuous learning and adaptation. Use online courses, workshops, and professional networks to build your skills and stay updated with the latest advancements. With dedication and the right approach, you can successfully integrate AI into your career and open up new opportunities for growth and advancement.

Career transformations with AI are not just about acquiring technical skills. They involve a mindset of continuous learning, adaptation, and resilience. Whether transitioning from data analysis to AI research or from marketing to AI consulting, the journey is filled with challenges and opportunities. By setting clear goals, seeking mentorship, and staying persistent, you can navigate this transformative path and achieve success in the exciting field of AI.

STAYING UPDATED WITH AI ADVANCEMENTS

Y ou're scrolling through a technology blog when an article on emerging AI trends catches your eye. What starts as casual browsing quickly turns into an exploration of the future of technology. This chapter will guide you through the latest developments in AI, ensuring you're always in the loop with what's new and exciting in this ever-evolving field.

7.1 EMERGING TRENDS IN AI: WHAT TO WATCH FOR

One of the most promising trends in AI is the rise of explainable AI (XAI). Traditionally AI models, in particular, deep learning ones, have been seen as black boxes. They produce results without providing much insight into how they arrived at those conclusions. Explainable AI aims to change that by making AI decisions transparent and understandable. In the case of a doctor using an AI tool to diagnose a condition, with XAI the AI can not only provide a diagnosis but also explain which symptoms and data points led to that conclusion. This transparency builds trust and allows humans to verify and understand AI decisions, which is crucial in fields like healthcare and finance, where stakes are high.

A significant trend is the expanding role of edge AI. Unlike traditional AI, which relies on cloud computing, edge AI processes data locally on devices. This approach reduces latency and enhances privacy, as data doesn't need to be sent to remote servers. Think of smart home devices that can make decisions without relying on constant internet connectivity. For example, a security camera that uses edge AI can instantly detect intruders and alert homeowners even if the internet is down. This decentralization of AI processing is particularly beneficial for applications requiring real-time responses, for example autonomous vehicles and industrial automation.

Advancements in AI ethics and governance frameworks are also shaping the future of artificial intelligence. As AI systems become a part of everyday life, the need for ethical guidelines and governance structures becomes critical. These frameworks ensure that AI is developed and used responsibly, addressing issues like bias, privacy and accountability. For example, IBM has pioneered in promoting ethical AI practices, establishing principles for transparency and fairness in AI development. These efforts are vital in ensuring that AI benefits society as a whole while minimizing potential harms.

The impact of these emerging trends is profound across various industries. As we have learned, in healthcare AI-driven personalized treatment plans are revolutionizing patient care. AI can analyze a patient's genetic makeup, lifestyle and medical history to recommend tailored treatments. This approach improves outcomes and reduces side effects by considering individual differences. In finance, AI-enhanced fraud detection and risk management systems are making transactions safer and more reliable. By analyzing patterns and detecting anomalies, these systems flag suspicious activities in real time, protecting both institutions and customers.

Retail is another sector undergoing significant transformation due to AI. AI-powered inventory management systems can predict demand, optimize stock levels and reduce waste. Customized retail experiences are also becoming the norm, with AI analyzing shopping behaviors to offer tailored recommendations.

Companies like Google AI (Gemini), NVIDIA, and IBM are leading the charge in these innovations. Google AI has made significant strides in explainable AI, developing tools that help users understand and trust machine learning models. NVIDIA is at the forefront of edge AI technologies, creating hardware and software solutions that enable efficient local processing. IBM's initiatives in ethical AI practices are setting standards for responsible AI development and ensuring fairness and transparency in AI systems.

Looking ahead, the future of these trends holds even more exciting possibilities. Adopting explainable AI is expected to increase across regulatory industries, providing clarity and trust in AI-driven decisions. Edge AI will likely expand further into IoT (Internet of Things) and smart devices, making everyday objects smarter and more responsive. As AI ethics and policies continue to strengthen, we can anticipate a more equitable and just integration of AI into society. These advancements promise a future where AI is not only more powerful but also more aligned with human values and needs.

7.2 QUANTUM COMPUTING AND AI: THE NEXT FRONTIER

What if your computer worked at lightning speed, solving problems that would take current machines years to figure out? Such is the promise of quantum computing. Unlike classical computers, which use bits as the smallest unit of data represented by 0s and 1s, quantum computers use qubits. A qubit can be both 0 and 1 simultaneously due to a property called superposition. This means quantum computers can process a massive number of possibilities at once. Another key concept is entanglement, where qubits become interconnected so that the state of one instantly influences the state of another no matter the distance between them. These features make quantum computing fundamentally different and immensely more powerful for specific tasks.

Now let's think about what quantum computing can do for AI. One of the most exciting potentials lies in accelerating machine learning model training. In classical computing, training complex models can be time-consuming, sometimes taking days or even weeks. Quantum computing can drastically reduce this time by efficiently handling vast amounts of data and computations so models can be trained faster, making developing and deploying AI solutions in various fields easier. Additionally, quantum computing excels at solving complex optimization problems. Think about logistics companies trying to find the most efficient routes for hundreds of delivery trucks. Quantum algorithms can evaluate countless possibilities in a fraction of the time, optimizing routes and saving resources.

Another significant benefit is in enhancing cryptographic security. Current encryption systems are vulnerable to quantum computing attacks but they can also create new, virtually unbreakable encryption This dual capability makes quantum computing a game-changer in cybersecurity. Quantum-enhanced cryptography could protect sensitive information far more effectively than today's standards ensuring data privacy and security in an era of increasing cyber threats.

Several leading tech companies are already exploring the synergy between quantum computing and AI. Google's Quantum AI lab is making strides in developing quantum algorithms that can outperform classical ones. Their research pushes the boundaries of what's possible, demonstrating quantum supremacy in specific tasks. IBM's Q Experience offers cloud-based access to quantum computers, giving researchers and developers the opportunity to experiment with quantum algorithms and explore their applications in AI. Microsoft Quantum Network is another initiative that connects researchers and organizations to advance quantum computing and its integration with AI. These projects highlight the collaborative effort to bring quantum AI from theory to practical reality.

Looking ahead, the implications of quantum AI are vast and transformative. Quantum-enhanced AI systems could outperform classical AI in numerous applications, from drug discovery to financial modeling. Imagine AI systems capable of simulating molecular interactions to develop new medications more quickly and accurately. In finance, quantum AI could optimize investment portfolios with unprecedented precision, uncovering patterns and trends that classical systems might miss. However, with these advancements come ethical and societal considerations. The immense power of quantum AI requires robust governance frameworks to ensure it's used responsibly. Issues like algorithmic bias, data privacy and equitable access to technology need to be addressed to avoid misuse and ensure that the benefits of quantum AI are distributed fairly.

7.3 AI IN SPACE EXPLORATION: REACHING FOR THE STARS

Imagine the vast expanse of space, where human presence is limited, and the need for precise decision-making is critical. AI is transforming space exploration by providing autonomous navigation and decision-making capabilities for spacecraft. These systems can make real-time adjustments to their trajectories, avoiding obstacles and optimizing fuel consumption without waiting for commands from Earth. This autonomy is especially crucial during long missions to distant planets, where communication delays can be significant. For example, NASA's Mars rovers use AI to navigate the Martian surface, deciding the best paths to take and identifying points of interest for further exploration.

Analyzing the huge quantities of data generated by space missions is another area where AI excels. Satellites and rovers collect massive datasets, including images, spectrometer readings and environmental metrics. AI algorithms process this data, identifying patterns and anomalies that can be missed by human analysts. The European Space Agency (ESA) employs AI to analyze satellite data, helping predict weather patterns and monitor environmental changes on Earth. This capability is essential for advancing our comprehension of planetary systems and improving our ability to respond to climate change and natural disasters.

AI-driven robotic explorers and assistants are also pivotal in space missions. Robots can take on tasks that would be too dangerous or monotonous for astronauts, such as repairing equipment, conducting scientific experiments, or even constructing habitats on other planets. SpaceX is exploring AI for autonomous spacecraft docking, a complex maneuver that requires precise calculations and adjustments. By automating this process, AI reduces the risk of human error and increases the efficiency of space operations.

The benefits of AI in space exploration are substantial. Reducing human intervention minimizes the risk of errors and enhances the safety of missions. AI enables real-time data processing and decision-making, which is critical for responding to unexpected challenges in space. For instance, during the Mars rover missions, AI systems analyze terrain data to avoid obstacles and select optimal routes, ensuring the rover safety and maximizing their scientific output. Additionally, AI enhances the accuracy of scientific discoveries by sifting through vast datasets to identify significant findings, such as potential signs of past life on Mars or the presence of valuable minerals.

Looking to the future, AI promises to shape the next era of space exploration in remarkable ways. Human missions to Mars and beyond will likely rely on AI for navigation, habitat management and scientific research. AI-based space habitats could autonomously regulate life support systems, monitor environmental conditions and perform maintenance tasks, ensuring the safety and well-being of astronauts. Collaboration between AI and astrophysics will deepen our understanding of the universe, enabling discoveries that are currently beyond our reach. For example, AI could assist in analyzing telescope data to identify exoplanets, study cosmic phenomena and even search for extraterrestrial intelligence.

We can envisage a future where AI-driven spacecraft are exploring the farthest reaches of our solar system, sending back data that expands our knowledge and challenges our understanding of the cosmos. AI could also play a crucial role in developing space infrastructure, such as building space stations, mining asteroids for resources and establishing colonies on other planets. These advancements will not only push the boundaries of human exploration but also open new frontiers for scientific research and technological innovation. As we continue to explore the stars, AI will be our indispensable partner, guiding us through the unknown and helping us uncover the secrets of the universe.

7.4 KEEPING UP WITH AI RESEARCH: RELIABLE RESOURCES

Browsing through bestseller titles in your favorite bookstore, it may occur to you that books helping you stay updated on the latest AI research would be a good read. AI research journals and publications are excellent resources. Journals like *The Journal of Artificial Intelligence Research (JAIR)*, *IEEE Transactions on Neural Networks and Learning Systems*, and *Machine Learning Journal* are reputable sources that publish groundbreaking studies and advancements in AI. These journals provide peer-reviewed articles that offer in-depth insights and detailed analyses, making them a goldmine for anyone serious about understanding the latest in AI.

Leading AI conferences and symposiums are another great way to stay current. Conferences like the *Neural Information Processing Systems (NeurIPS)*, *International Conference on Machine Learning (ICML)*, and *Conference on Computer Vision and Pattern Recognition (CVPR)* gather top researchers and practitioners to present their latest findings. These events are informative and provide opportunities network and learn from experts in the field. Attending these conferences, whether in person or virtually, can give you firsthand exposure to cutting-edge research and emerging trends.

Online platforms and repositories for AI research papers are invaluable. Websites like *arXiv* and *Google Scholar* offer free access to various research papers. ArXiv, in particular, is a preprint repository where researchers upload their papers before they are peer-reviewed, providing early access to the latest studies. Google Scholar enables you to search for articles, theses, books and conference papers, often providing links to full-text versions. These platforms make it easy to find and read the latest research, ensuring you stay abreast of new developments.

Influential AI research organizations and institutions are at the forefront of AI advancements. OpenAI for example, has been a trailblazer in AI research, known for developing models like GPT-3, which powers many natural language processing applications. Google's DeepMind has made headlines with its groundbreaking studies, including AlphaGo, which defeated human champions in the complex game of Go. MIT's Computer Science and Artificial Intelligence Laboratory (CSAIL) is another powerhouse, driving innovation in areas like robotics, machine learning and AI ethics. These organizations publish their research findings, making their websites and publications valuable resources for anyone interested in AI.

Reading and understanding AI research papers can seem daunting, but with the right approach, it becomes manageable. Start by identifying key sections: the abstract, methodology, results and conclusion. The abstract summarizes the research, giving you a quick overview. The methodology explains how the research was conducted, which is crucial for understanding the validity of the findings. The results section presents the data and outcomes, while the conclusion summarizes the implications of the research. Summarize these findings and implications in your own words to deepen your understanding. Use online tools and forums like ResearchGate and Reddit's r/MachineLearning for discussions and clarifications. These platforms allow you to engage with other readers and sometimes even the authors, providing deeper insights into the research.

Engaging with the AI research community can significantly enhance your learning. Joining AI research forums and discussion groups like AI Alignment Forum or the AI section on Stack Exchange allows you to interact with peers and experts. Participating in AI hackathons and research competitions, such as those hosted by Kaggle, offers hands-on experience and the chance to solve real-world problems while allowing you to test your skills against others. Attending webinars and workshops by AI researchers can also be incredibly beneficial. These events usually feature presentations on the latest research and developments, providing you with direct access to cutting-edge knowledge and the opportunity to ask questions and engage in discussions.

By taking advantage of these resources and participating in the AI community, you can stay updated on the latest advancements and deepen your understanding of this rapidly advancing subject.

7.5 CONTINUOUS LEARNING: INTEGRATING AI INTO YOUR LIFE

Walking through a tech expo, you are surrounded by the latest gadgets and innovations. To navigate this ever-changing landscape, continuous learning is not just beneficial—it's essential. AI is a field that evolves rapidly, with new technologies and methodologies emerging constantly. By staying updated, you enhance your career opportunities, making yourself valuable in a competitive job market. Companies seek individuals who can bring innovative AI solutions to the table, driving progress and efficiency. Continuous learning ensures you stay ahead, contributing to advancements that can reshape industries and improve lives.

Integrating AI learning into your daily routine doesn't have to be overwhelming. Start by making time for learning and practice. Treat it like any other important task on your schedule. Whether it's 30 minutes in the morning before work or an hour on the weekends, consistency is key. Mobile apps and online courses offer flexibility, allowing you to learn on the go.

To keep your AI knowledge current, explore a variety of resources. Online courses and MOOCs (Massive Open Online Courses) are excellent for structured learning. They often contain interactive elements, assignments, and quizzes that reinforce your knowledge. Podcasts and YouTube channels dedicated to AI can provide insights and updates in a more casual format. Listening to AI podcasts during your commute or watching YouTube tutorials can turn idle time into productive learning sessions. AI-focused blogs and newsletters are another great way to stay informed. Subscribe to a few reputable sources to make sure you receive regular updates on the latest trends and breakthroughs.

Practical experience is vital in mastering AI. Working on personal AI projects allows you to apply what you've learned and experiment with different techniques. Start with small projects such as those I have described. Then, as you gain confidence, you can tackle more complex challenges. Contributing to open-source AI projects is another excellent way to gain hands-on experience. Platforms like GitHub host numerous projects where you can collaborate with others, learn from experienced developers, and contribute to real-world applications. Participating in AI competitions and challenges (think Kaggle) is a good way to simulate real-world problems, giving you a taste of how AI is applied in various industries.

In summary, continuous learning in AI is not only about keeping up with the latest technologies; it's about actively engaging with them. By setting aside time for learning, using flexible resources, and gaining practical experience, you can seamlessly integrate AI into your life. This approach enhances your career prospects and positions you as a contributor to innovative AI solutions, driving progress in this exciting field.

8

REAL-WORLD APPLICATIONS OF AI

I magine being in a hospital where doctors use advanced technology to diagnose diseases faster and more accurately than ever thought possible. A world where AI systems analyze medical images and patient data, providing insights that save lives. You'd be forgiven for thinking this was a scene from a sci-fi movie, but in fact, it is the reality of AI in healthcare today. The integration of AI in medicine is revolutionizing how we approach diagnostics, treatment plans, and patient care, making healthcare more efficient and personalized.

8.1 AI IN HEALTHCARE: REVOLUTIONIZING MEDICINE

AI's role in medical diagnostics is nothing short of revolutionary. A radiologist examines a stack of X-rays to detect anomalies such as tumors. Traditionally this process has been time-consuming and sometimes prone to error. AI-powered image analysis changes this by using advanced algorithms to scan diagnostic images for abnormalities. These systems can interpret images with remarkable accuracy, often identifying signs that might be missed by the human eye.

Predictive analytics is another area in which AI shines in early disease detection. By analyzing vast quantities of patient data, AI systems can predict the likelihood of conditions such as diabetes and heart disease before symptoms even appear. This predictive capability allows for early intervention, potentially preventing severe health issues. For example, AI algorithms analyze patterns in medical files to identify patients at risk of developing chronic diseases, enabling healthcare providers to offer preventive measures and personalized care plans.

Thanks to AI, personalized medicine tailored to individual patients is increasingly within reach. One of the most promising applications is in genomic analysis for cancer treatment. AI systems analyze genetic information to identify specific mutations in a patient's DNA, allowing doctors to effectively tailor treatments that target these mutations. This has the huge benefit of improving the odds of successful outcomes and minimizing side effects. Additionally, AI-driven drug discovery accelerates the development of new medications. By simulating how different compounds interact with biological targets, AI speeds up the identification of promising drugs, reducing the time and cost to bring new treatments to market.

AI also has a significant role in patient care and management. Wearable health monitors equipped with AI provide real-time data to healthcare providers, ensuring continuous monitoring of patients' vital signs. These devices can alert doctors to potential issues before they become critical, allowing for timely interventions. Virtual health assistants further enhance patient care by managing appointments, medication reminders, and providing health information. These AI-driven assistants ensure that patients adhere to their treatment plans and monitor their own health, ultimately improving outcomes.

Case studies illustrate the real benefits of AI in healthcare. Google's DeepMind collaboration with British doctors led to the development of an AI system for diagnosing eye diseases. This system, capable of identifying 50 different eye conditions, uses dual neural networks to translate raw OCT scans into tissue maps and analyze them for symptoms. The transparency of this system which shows its diagnostic process, distinguishes it from other AI systems like IBM's Watson for Oncology, which has faced criticism for a lack of clarity. DeepMind's system addresses specialist shortages, particularly in eye care, by automating diagnosis and triage, reducing patient wait times and improving outcomes.

IBM Watson analyzes vast datasets of medical literature, clinical trial data and patient records to provide oncologists with evidence-based treatment recommendations. This AI system helps doctors identify the most effective treatment options for individual patients, considering the latest research and clinical guidelines. Watson's ability to process and analyze massive amounts of data quickly ensures that patients receive the most up-to-date and personalized care possible.

The integration of AI in healthcare is not just a technological advancement. It is a paradigm shift that enhances the capabilities of medical professionals, making healthcare more efficient, accurate and personalized. The future of medicine is here, and it is powered by AI.

8.2 AI IN FINANCE: ENHANCING DECISION-MAKING

No one wants the unpleasant surprise of logging into their banking app and seeing an alert about a suspicious transaction, but unfortunately it happens. A real-time alert is possible because of AI's role in fraud detection. AI systems analyze transaction patterns to identify anomalies that might indicate fraudulent activities. These machine-learning models can scan through vast amounts of transaction data, looking for unusual patterns that deviate from a customer's typical behavior. For instance, if your account suddenly shows a large purchase in a foreign country while your spending history is mostly local, the AI flags this as suspicious. These models continuously learn and adapt, improving their accuracy over time. The resulting real-time alerts help banks and credit card companies prevent fraud before it impacts customers, safeguarding both finances and personal information.

In the high-speed world of stock trading, AI has revolutionized algorithmic trading. High-frequency trading algorithms powered by AI make split-second decisions that humans cannot match. These algorithms analyze market data, identify trends and execute trades within milliseconds. This speed and efficiency allow traders to capitalize on market movements instantly. Additionally, AI-driven portfolio management optimizes investment strategies by balancing risk and reward. By examining past trends and present market dynamics AI systems can recommend the best mix of assets to meet an investor's goals. This optimization ensures that portfolios are well-diversified and positioned to maximize returns while minimizing risks.

Credit scoring and risk management are other critical areas AI significantly impacts. Traditional credit scoring methods rely on limited data points such as credit history and income. AI, however, can analyze alternative data sources to provide a more accurate assessment of creditworthiness. For example, AI can consider factors like utility payments, social media activity, and even mobile phone usage patterns. This comprehensive analysis creates a more inclusive credit scoring system, enabling lenders to make better-informed decisions. Predictive models also play an important role in assessing loan default risks. By analyzing a borrower's financial behavior and market trends, AI can predict the likelihood of default, allowing lenders to take proactive measures to lessen risks.

One of the standout examples of AI in financial services is JPMorgan Chase's COIN platform. This AI-powered system automates the document review process for business credit agreements. Traditionally, this task would take thousands of hours annually. COIN, however, completes it in seconds. The platform uses unassisted AI and image recognition to compare and identify different contract clauses, extracting relevant attributes. This automation saves time and costs and reduces errors, ensuring greater accuracy and efficiency in contract management.

PayPal's use of AI for fraud detection further illustrates the technology's benefits. PayPal processes millions of transactions daily, making it a prime target for fraudsters. To combat this, PayPal employs AI to monitor and analyze transactions in real time. The AI system identifies suspicious activities, such as unusual login attempts or rapid transactions across multiple accounts. This proactive approach enables PayPal to prevent fraudulent activities before they affect users, maintaining trust and security on the platform.

These case studies highlight how AI enhances decision-making in finance. From fraud detection to algorithmic trading, credit scoring and risk management, AI brings efficiency, accuracy and security to financial services. As AI evolves, its role in finance will undoubtedly expand, offering even more sophisticated tools and solutions to meet the industry's needs.

8.3 AI IN ENTERTAINMENT: TRANSFORMING MEDIA AND GAMING

Think of watching a movie where every scene flows perfectly, the music enhances every moment and the storyline captivates you from start to finish. AI plays a crucial part in making this a seamless experience. In the realm of content creation, AI-generated scripts and music compositions are pushing the boundaries of creativity. These AI systems analyze unimaginable amounts of existing scripts and musical pieces to generate new, original content. For instance, an AI might study hundreds of movie scripts to understand plot structures, character development and dialogue patterns. It then uses this knowledge to create a script that feels fresh yet familiar. Similarly, AI can compose music by learning from various genres and styles, producing compositions that resonate with audiences.

Automated video editing and special effects generation are other areas where AI shines. Traditionally, video editing is a labor-intensive process that requires a keen eye for detail. AI simplifies this by automatically cutting, splicing and enhancing video footage. For example, if you're creating a highlight reel of a sports event, AI can identify the most exciting moments and stitch them together seamlessly. Special effects generation too, benefits from AI's precision and efficiency. AI algorithms can add realistic effects to scenes, such as explosions, weather changes, or even transforming actors into fantastical creatures. This saves time and elevates the quality of the final product.

Personalized recommendations have become a staple of modern entertainment platforms thanks to AI. Streaming services like Netflix and Spotify use complex recommendation engines to curate content tailored to individual users. These engines analyze your viewing or listening habits, such as the genres you prefer, the time you spend on different types of content, and your interactions with various shows or songs. Based on this data, AI predicts what you might enjoy next and presents personalized suggestions. This keeps you engaged and ensures you always have something new and interesting to watch or listen to. Social media platforms also leverage AI to suggest content that aligns with your interests, enhancing your overall experience.

In the gaming industry, AI significantly enhances player experiences and game development. AI-driven non-playable characters (NPCs) interact dynamically, making games more immersive and engaging. These NPCs can adapt to players' actions, offering more realistic and challenging gameplay. For instance, in a role-playing game, an AI-driven NPC might change its behavior based on your character's decisions, creating a unique experience for each player. Procedural content generation is another exciting application of AI in gaming. This technique uses algorithms to develop game environments, levels, and even entire worlds dynamically. Instead of pre-designed levels, AI generates new and unique settings each time you play, ensuring that no two gaming experiences are the same.

Case studies highlight the revolutionary impact of AI in entertainment. For example, Netflix uses AI to personalize viewing experiences and optimize content production. On the other hand, Ubisoft applies AI to enhance dynamic gameplay experiences. The company's AI systems analyze player behavior to create adaptive NPCs and procedurally generated environments, making games more engaging and replayable.

AI's integration into entertainment enhances the quality and creativity of content and personalizes and enriches the user experience. Whether watching a movie, listening to music, or playing a game, AI ensures that the experience is tailored to your preferences and continually evolving.

8.4 SMART HOMES: INTEGRATING AI INTO DAILY LIFE

Waking up to a house that adjusts itself to your daily routine is a current reality. AI-powered home automation systems make this possible by learning your preferences and habits. Take smart thermostats like the Nest, for instance. These devices learn your temperature preferences and modify the heating and cooling accordingly. Over time they optimize energy use, making your home more comfortable as well as saving on utility bills. AI-driven lighting systems are another marvel. They adapt to your habits and natural light levels, ensuring that lights are only on when needed. This creates a pleasant ambiance and contributes to energy efficiency.

Safety is a paramount concern for any home and AI enhances security and surveillance in remarkable ways. AI-powered security cameras equipped with facial recognition and anomaly detection can identify familiar faces and alert you to unknown visitors. They can detect unusual activities around your home and send real-time alerts, giving you peace of mind. Smart doorbells like Ring take this further by providing video feeds and notifications whenever someone approaches your door. You can see and speak to visitors even when you're not home, enhancing security and convenience.

Personal assistants like Amazon Alexa and Google Home have become indispensable for daily tasks. These AI-powered devices can handle various functions, from setting reminders and managing schedules to controlling other smart home devices. Need a quick recipe suggestion? AI-enabled kitchen appliances can offer just that. These smart gadgets can suggest recipes based on your ingredients, guide you through cooking steps, and even adjust your oven or stove settings for optimal results.

Consider a case study of a fully integrated smart home ecosystem. In this home, every device communicates seamlessly through a central AI hub. The smart thermostat adjusts the temperature according to time of day and who's at home, reducing energy consumption. AI-driven lighting systems dim or brighten according to natural light and user presence, creating an energy-efficient environment. Security is bolstered with AI-powered cameras and smart locks, which not only detect intruders but also recognize family members and frequent visitors. This setup enhances comfort and security and significantly lowers energy bills.

In another real-world example, a homeowner uses AI-driven home automation to improve their quality of life. Mornings start with the smart coffee maker brewing the perfect cup as the bedroom lights gradually brighten to simulate sunrise. Throughout the day, AI manages the home's climate control, keeping the environment comfortable without wasting energy. Security cameras monitor the property, sending alerts if any unusual activity is detected. In the kitchen, an AI-enabled refrigerator suggests meal plans based on the stored ingredients, reducing food waste. This level of automation frees up time and mental energy, allowing the homeowner to focus on more important tasks.

These smart home technologies are not just about convenience; they represent a shift towards more efficient, secure, and sustainable living. AI integration in daily home management simplifies tasks, enhances security, and contributes to a greener environment by optimizing resource use.

8.5 AI IN RETAIL: PERSONALIZING CUSTOMER EXPERIENCES

Wouldn't we love to walk into a store where every product seems tailored to your tastes? This is the magic of AI in personalized shopping experiences. E-commerce platforms use AI to analyze your browsing history, purchasing patterns, and even the time you spend looking at certain items. This data-driven approach allows AI to recommend products that align with your preferences. For instance, when you shop on Amazon, the "Recommended for You" section is powered by AI algorithms that predict what you might like based on your past behavior. These personalized recommendations improve your shopping experience by making it easier to find products that match your interests, ultimately increasing both satisfaction and sales.

AI-driven marketing campaigns take personalization a step further. Retailers use AI to create targeted ads that resonate with individual customers. By analyzing data such as your previous purchases, browsing history, even social media activity, AI can compose marketing messages that are specifically tailored to your needs and preferences. This targeted approach makes it more likely that the ads you see are relevant, increasing the likelihood of a purchase. For example, if you recently bought a pair of running shoes, AI might suggest related products like athletic wear or fitness trackers in future marketing emails.

As well as enhancing the shopping experience, AI significantly improves inventory management and supply chain optimization. Predictive analytics allow retailers to forecast inventory needs accurately, reducing the risk of over or under-stocking. By analyzing historical sales data, present market trends, and even weather patterns, AI can predict which products will be in demand and when.

This helps retailers maintain optimal inventory levels, reducing costs and keeping customers happy. AI algorithms also optimize supply chain logistics by determining the most efficient routes for shipping and identifying potential bottlenecks. This efficiency makes sure that products reach customers quickly and cost-effectively.

Customer service is another area where AI makes a substantial impact. AI-powered chatbots and virtual assistants provide 24/7 support, answering customer questions and resolving problems in real time. As we have seen, chatbots use natural language processing to understand and respond to customer questions, offering a seamless and efficient experience. For instance, if you have a question about a product's availability, a chatbot can quickly check the inventory and provide an answer. Additionally, sentiment analysis tools help retailers understand customer feedback by analyzing reviews and social media posts. These tools identify common themes and sentiments, enabling retailers to address concerns and improve their service.

Practical examples illustrate the transformative power of AI in retail. Amazon is a prime example of a company that leverages AI for personalized shopping experiences and efficient logistics. Amazon's AI algorithms analyze vast amounts of customer data to recommend products, personalize the shopping experience, and optimize inventory management. This data-driven approach ensures that customers find what they need quickly and easily, enhancing their overall shopping experience. Another notable example is Zara, which uses AI to manage its inventory and forecast fashion trends. By analyzing sales data, customer feedback, and social media trends, Zara's AI system predicts which styles will be popular in the coming seasons. This allows Zara to produce and stock the right products, reducing waste and meeting customer demand more effectively.

Integrating AI in retail revolutionizes how businesses operate and interact with customers. Personalized recommendations, targeted marketing campaigns, optimized inventory management, and enhanced customer service are just a few of the many benefits AI brings to the retail industry. These advancements improve efficiency and profitability and create a more fun and personalized shopping experience for customers.

AI's role in retail is only one of the many ways this technology is transforming industries. From healthcare to finance, entertainment to daily living, AI's impact is profound and far-reaching. As we continue to explore AI's possibilities, it becomes clear that its potential is limitless.

9

ETHICAL CONSIDERATIONS IN AI

J ust think how you'd feel if you were about to withdraw some cash from an ATM only to be denied with no clear explanation. You later discover that the AI system managing your bank's transactions flagged your account for potential fraud based on the neighborhood you live in. This small but impactful inconvenience stems from a deeper issue: bias in AI systems. As AI technologies become more integrated into our lives, understanding and addressing bias in these systems becomes essential.

9.1 UNDERSTANDING BIAS IN AI: CAUSES AND SOLUTIONS

Bias in AI systems originates from multiple sources, primarily incomplete or unrepresentative datasets and historical biases that reflect societal prejudices. When training data doesn't represent the real world's diversity, AI models can produce skewed results. For instance, if an AI system is trained on a dataset primarily made up of images of particular racial characteristics, it will struggle to recognize or interpret images of individuals outside this demographic accurately. This inadequate representation can lead to biased outcomes, even if the algorithms themselves are technically sound.

Historical biases embedded in data also play a significant role. Societal prejudices, whether explicit or implicit, can be captured in datasets and perpetuated by AI systems. For example, hiring algorithms trained on historical employment data favor male candidates over female ones if the original dataset reflects a male-dominated workforce. This perpetuates gender biases and can result in discriminatory hiring practices and limiting job opportunities for qualified candidates, even if unintentional. Similarly, facial recognition technology has been shown to have higher error rates for women and people from diverse ethnic backgrounds, leading to potential misidentifications and wrongful accusations.

The impact of bias in AI is profound and far-reaching. In criminal justice, biased AI systems used for risk assessments can disproportionately label individuals from certain racial or socioeconomic backgrounds as high-risk, leading to unfair treatment and sentencing. These biases can undermine trust in AI systems and exacerbate social inequalities.

Several strategies can be employed to combat bias in AI. Fairness-aware machine learning techniques aim to design algorithms that minimize bias and promote fairness. One approach is to use diverse datasets during the training phase, ensuring that the AI system learns from a broad spectrum of examples. Regular auditing and testing of AI models for bias is also essential. By continuously evaluating the performance of AI systems and identifying any biases that emerge, developers can make necessary adjustments to improve fairness.

Case studies highlight the importance of addressing bias. One notable example is the COMPAS system used for criminal justice risk assessments. Studies have shown that COMPAS is biased against African-American defendants, often labeling them as higher risk compared to their white counterparts. Efforts to mitigate this bias include re-evaluating the datasets used for training and incorporating fairness constraints into the algorithm. In healthcare, an AI system designed to predict mortality rates was found to be biased against African-American patients. By revising the training data to include a more diverse patient population and regularly auditing the system's performance, developers were able to reduce the bias and improve the system's accuracy.

Addressing bias in AI is not just a technical challenge but a societal imperative. By understanding the origins of bias and implementing strategies to mitigate it, we can create AI systems that are fairer and more inclusive. This ensures that the benefits of AI are available to anyone, regardless of their background or circumstances.

9.2 PRIVACY CONCERNS: HOW AI HANDLES YOUR DATA

Every day, as you scroll through social media, use your smartphone, or make online purchases, AI systems are covertly collecting and analyzing your data. This data comes from various sources like social media posts, sensor readings from smart devices, and transaction records from your online activities. These data points are invaluable for training AI models and improving their accuracy. For instance, your browsing history helps recommendation engines suggest products you might like, while your location data can optimize navigation apps to offer the fastest route to your destination.

However, the collection and use of this data come with significant privacy risks. One major concern is surveillance. AI-powered cameras and facial recognition systems can monitor your movements and activities, raising questions about how this data is stored and who can access it. Another risk is security breaches. Unauthorized access to your private information can lead to identity theft and financial loss. Recent incidents have shown that even well-protected systems are not immune to cyber-attacks, making the need for robust privacy measures more critical than ever.

To protect your privacy, several techniques have been developed. Differential privacy adds noise to the data, ensuring that individual identities are masked while allowing useful patterns to be extracted. Think of it as blurring the fine details in a photograph while keeping the overall image clear. Another method, federated learning, trains AI models across multiple devices without centralizing the data. Your data stays on your device, and only the learning updates are shared, reducing the risk of exposure. This technique is especially useful for applications like predictive text, where your typing habits help improve the model without compromising your privacy.

Real-world scenarios highlight the balance between AI utility and privacy. Retail companies, for example, use AI to deliver targeted advertising. By analyzing your purchase history and browsing patterns, they can suggest products that match your preferences. However, they must also implement privacy-preserving techniques to ensure your data isn't misused or exposed. In healthcare, privacy is paramount. Healthcare providers use AI systems to analyze patient data for better diagnostics and treatment plans. To protect sensitive medical information, they employ privacy-preserving AI techniques like differential privacy and secure multi-party computation, which allows collaborative analysis without revealing individual patient data.

Consider the case of a healthcare provider using AI to predict patient outcomes. By applying federated learning, they can train their models on data from multiple hospitals without ever centralizing the information. Each hospital's data remains secure, and the AI system benefits from a more diverse dataset, improving its predictive accuracy. This approach enhances patient care and builds trust, as patients know their data is being used responsibly.

Understanding how AI handles your data and the measures taken to protect your privacy is vital in today's digital age. By being aware of these practices, you can better appreciate the balance between technological advancements and the safeguarding of personal information.

9.3 AI AND JOB DISPLACEMENT: NAVIGATING THE FUTURE OF WORK

Picturing a factory where robots efficiently assemble products with precision and speed might seem unrealistic but this scene highlights a significant shift in the workforce due to automation and AI. Industries like manufacturing, retail and transportation are particularly affected. In manufacturing, robots perform tasks that once required human hands, from assembling cars to packaging goods. Retail sees AI-driven inventory management systems replacing manual stock checks, while in transportation, self-driving vehicles threaten to displace truck drivers and delivery personnel.

Predictions about the job market suggest that AI will continue to automate repetitive tasks, potentially displacing millions of jobs. However, this isn't the end of the story. AI also creates new opportunities. While some roles may vanish, others will emerge, and jobs in AI development, maintenance and oversight are on the rise. These roles require skills in programming, data analysis and machine learning. Additionally, new fields like AI ethics and policymaking are gaining importance. As AI systems become integrated into society, ethical and responsible use becomes crucial which creates demand for professionals who can navigate the moral and regulatory landscapes of AI.

Continuous learning and upskilling are vital to prepare for these changes. Workers need to adapt by acquiring new skills that complement AI technologies. Government and corporate initiatives play a significant role in this transition. Programs focused on reskilling and upskilling can help workers stay relevant in the job market. For example, tech companies offer online courses and workshops to teach employees about AI and machine learning. Governments can support these efforts with funding and policy frameworks encouraging lifelong learning.

Consider the experience of a large automotive manufacturer. Initially, introducing AI-driven robots led to job cuts on the assembly line. However, the company also invested in training programs for its workforce. Employees learned to maintain and program the new robots, transitioning into more technical roles. This shift not only saved jobs but also improved job satisfaction and pay. Similarly, in the realm of AI ethics, organizations like Google and Microsoft have established dedicated teams to oversee the ethical use of AI. These teams work to ensure AI systems are developed and deployed responsibly, creating new career paths for those interested in the intersection of technology and ethics.

The work landscape is changing rapidly with the emergence of AI. While automation creates challenges, it also opens up new avenues for career growth and innovation. By focusing on continuous education and adapting to new roles, individuals can successfully navigate this transformation.

9.4 THE ROLE OF AI IN SOCIAL EQUITY

The dual impact of AI on social equity is profound. On one hand, AI can potentially reinforce social inequalities through biased algorithms. When left unchecked, these systems can perpetuate existing disparities. However, AI also holds promise for promoting social equity. Numerous initiatives leverage AI for positive social change. For example, AI-powered personalized learning platforms are bridging the achievement gap in education. These systems analyze individual learning patterns to tailor educational content, helping students from diverse backgrounds achieve their full potential. In healthcare, AI is improving access to medical services in underserved areas. Telemedicine platforms supported by AI enable remote diagnosis and treatment, bringing quality healthcare to communities that previously had limited access. In the criminal justice system, work is underway to use AI to reduce bias and improve fairness. By re-evaluating risk assessment tools and ensuring they are trained on diverse datasets, AI can support more equitable decision-making processes.

Inclusive AI development is necessary to realize the positive potential of AI. Diversity in AI research and development teams is key in reducing bias. When teams include individuals from various backgrounds, they bring different perspectives that can identify and address potential biases. For example, an inclusive team working on a facial recognition project will more likely create a system that accurately recognizes people of all skin tones. Projects that prioritize inclusivity create fairer AI systems and produce outcomes that better serve all users. A notable example is the development of an AI tool designed to assist visually impaired individuals. By involving visually impaired developers and users in the design process, the team created a tool that genuinely met the needs of its intended audience.

Real life examples further illustrate the impact of AI on social equity. One case study involves an AI-driven initiative providing legal assistance to low-income individuals. This initiative uses natural language processing to analyze legal documents and offer preliminary advice, making legal services more accessible to those who cannot afford traditional legal representation. Another example is AI programs improving access to education for disadvantaged communities. Using AI to identify and support at-risk students, these programs offer personalized interventions that help students stay on track and succeed academically. These initiatives demonstrate how AI can be a powerful tool for promoting fairness and justice when developed and applied thoughtfully.

The dual nature of AI's impact on social equity underscores the importance of responsible development and deployment. While AI can reinforce existing inequalities if left unchecked, it also has the potential to drive significant positive change. By prioritizing inclusivity and leveraging AI for social good, we can harness its power to create a more equitable and just society.

9.5 ETHICAL FRAMEWORKS FOR RESPONSIBLE AI DEVELOPMENT

By now, it's clear that we inhabit a world where AI systems make decisions that significantly impact our daily lives, from the job offers we receive to the medical treatments we are recommended. In such a world, we need to be sure beyond doubt that these AI systems operate ethically. Key principles like fairness, accountability, transparency and privacy form the backbone of ethical AI development. Organizations like IEEE and the European Commission have laid out guidelines to ensure these principles are upheld. Fairness involves AI systems that do not discriminate against individuals based on race, gender, or socioeconomic status.

Accountability holds developers and organizations responsible for the actions and decisions made by AI systems. Transparency involves making AI processes understandable to non-experts. Privacy protects individuals' data so that it is used responsibly and securely.

Ethical frameworks play a crucial role in AI governance by providing a structured approach to regulate AI development and deployment. These frameworks guide organizations in implementing ethical principles throughout the AI lifecycle, from start to finish. Ethical oversight is vital in AI projects to prevent misuse and ensure that AI systems align with societal values.

Implementing ethical AI involves several practical steps. Organizations can start by conducting ethical impact assessments to identify potential ethical problems and develop strategies to address them. This involves evaluating how AI systems might affect different groups of people and ensuring that these impacts are considered in the design and deployment phases. Incorporating ethics into AI development lifecycles ensures that ethical considerations are an intrinsic part of the development process. Engaging stakeholders and communities in AI governance is also crucial. By involving a diverse group of people, including anyone directly affected by AI systems, organizations can gain valuable insights and build AI systems that are more equitable and inclusive.

Several organizations have successfully implemented ethical AI practices. A notable example is a tech company that has integrated ethical guidelines into its AI development process. This company conducts regular ethical reviews, engages with diverse stakeholders, and ensures transparency in its AI systems. By doing so, it builds trust with its users and sets a standard for ethical AI development. Another example is the government's approach to regulating AI with ethical guidelines. By establishing clear regulations and ethical standards, the government ensures that AI systems used within its jurisdiction are fair, accountable and respect individual rights. This approach protects citizens and promotes the responsible development of AI technologies.

As we wrap up this chapter, it's clear that we need ethical frameworks guiding the responsible development and deployment of AI. By adhering to principles like fairness, accountability, transparency, and privacy and implementing practical strategies, we can ensure that AI systems benefit everyone. Ethical AI is not just theoretical. It's an absolute necessity for building a future where technology serves humanity responsibly and equitably.

AI TOOLS AND RESOURCES

This chapter is your guide through the wide variety of AI platforms. It is designed to fire up your curiosity and enhance your skills. Each of these offers unique capabilities that can help you immerse yourself in the world of artificial intelligence, no matter your background or level of expertise.

10.1 POPULAR AI PLATFORMS: A COMPARATIVE GUIDE

Let's explore some of the most widely used platforms and understand their unique offerings.

When it comes to ease of use, Google Colab stands out for its simplicity and ease of setup, making it a fantastic starting point for anyone new to AI. It's a free cloud-based Jupyter Notebook environment that allows you to write and execute Python code in your browser with no setup required. Its integration with Google Drive means you can easily store and share your projects, making collaboration straightforward. One standout feature of Google Colab'is its free access to GPUs, which significantly speeds up the training of machine learning models. This platform is ideal for beginners, students and educators looking for an accessible entry point into AI without the need for powerful local hardware.

AWS SageMaker offers a comprehensive suite for building, training and deploying machine learning models at scale. It smoothly integrates with other Amazon Web Services (AWS), making it a powerful tool for professionals already invested in the AWS ecosystem. SageMaker provides built-in algorithms and managed services that simplify the complex process of model development. Although there's a learning curve, especially for those new to AWS, the platform's extensive documentation and community support can help ease the transition. SageMaker's scalability makes it suitable for both small experiments and large enterprise-level projects.

Microsoft Azure Machine Learning is another robust cloud service designed for machine learning. Its seamless integration with other Microsoft services, such as Azure DevOps and Power BI, provides a cohesive environment for developing and deploying AI solutions. Azure Machine Learning supports a range of programming languages and frameworks, offering flexibility to developers. Its user-friendly interface and comprehensive set of tools make it accessible to both beginners and experienced professionals. However, the pricing can add up quickly, especially for extensive use, so monitoring usage closely is essential.

IBM Watson is renowned for its advanced natural language processing (NLP) capabilities, making it a go-to platform for businesses intending to leverage AI for language-related tasks. Watson offers a suite of AI services and applications designed to solve business challenges, from customer service automation to data insights. Its unique selling point is the ability to understand and process human language with high accuracy, thanks to its sophisticated NLP algorithms. While Watson can be more complex to set up than other platforms, its powerful tools and applications make it a useful resource for businesses looking to implement AI solutions.

To help you get started, here's a practical example of setting up a project in Google Colab. First, visit the Google Colab website and sign in with your Google account. Click on "New Notebook" to create a new project. You'll see a code cell where you can start writing Python code. For instance, you can import necessary libraries like TensorFlow or PyTorch to train a simple machine-learning model directly into the notebook. Google Colab provides free GPU access, which you can enable by going to "Runtime" > "Change runtime type" and selecting "GPU" as the hardware accelerator. This setup allows you to execute intensive computations quickly and efficiently.

Setting up a machine learning model using AWS SageMaker begins with logging into the AWS Management Console and navigating to SageMaker. Create a new notebook instance by choosing "Notebook instances" and clicking "Create notebook instance." Configure the instance with a name, instance type and IAM role. Once your instance is ready, you can open Jupyter, a web-based notebook environment, and start writing your code. SageMaker provides built-in algorithms for training models, which you can access through the SageMaker SDK in Python. Train your model, evaluate its performance, and deploy it directly from the notebook interface.

For those using Microsoft Azure, start by logging in to the Azure portal and creating a new Machine Learning workspace. In the workspace, create a new experiment and choose your preferred programming environment, such as Jupyter Notebook. Azure Machine Learning provides pre-configured environments for data preprocessing, which you can use to clean and prepare your datasets. Write your code to train and test machine learning models, utilizing Azure's powerful computing resources. Once your model is ready, deploy it as a web service with just a few clicks, making it accessible for applications and users.

To implement a chatbot with IBM Watson, begin by logging in to IBM Cloud and creating a Watson Assistant service. Configure your assistant by defining intents (user goals) and entities (specific data points) that the bot should recognize. Use Watson's intuitive interface to build dialog flows, ensuring your chatbot can handle various user interactions. Once your chatbot is built, integrate it with your website or application using IBM Watson's APIs. Watson's advanced NLP capabilities will enable your chatbot to understand and respond to user queries appropriately, providing a hassle-free user experience.

These platforms offer a variety of functions to accommodate different needs, from beginners looking for an easy entry point to professionals seeking powerful tools for complex projects. Each platform has unique strengths and potential flaws, but understanding these can help you choose the best one for your AI endeavors.

10.2 ONLINE COURSES AND TUTORIALS: WHERE TO LEARN MORE

Ready to explore AI but uncertain about where to begin? The internet offers many courses designed to guide you through this fascinating field. One of the best places to begin is Coursera, where you can find "Machine Learning" by Andrew Ng. This course is renowned for its strong focus on foundational concepts and practical applications. Andrew Ng's teaching style is clear and engaging, making complex topics accessible. The course covers essential algorithms, data preprocessing and model evaluation, providing a solid base for further exploration.

If you're looking for something even more accessible, edX offers "AI for Everyone" also by Andrew Ng. This is the perfect course if you have no prior knowledge of AI. It breaks down AI concepts into bite-sized, understandable segments, emphasizing the impact of AI on society and various industries. Unlike more technical courses, "AI for Everyone" focuses on AI literacy, making it ideal for business leaders, policymakers and anyone curious about how AI can be applied in different contexts.

For a more immersive experience, the "Deep Learning Nanodegree" on Udacity offers a comprehensive curriculum with hands-on projects. This course delves deeper into neural networks, convolutional networks and recurrent networks. You'll be able to work on real-world problems, applying what you've learned to projects like image classification and language modeling. The Nanodegree program is structured to provide a blend of theory and practice, with support from mentors and a vibrant community of learners.

Khan Academy is another excellent resource, particularly for those who prefer free and easy-to-understand lessons. Their introductory AI and machine learning courses cover the basics, such as linear regression and clustering, using simple language and clear examples. The platform's interactive exercises reinforce your learning, making it easier to grasp fundamental concepts.

Choosing the right course depends on several factors. First, consider the content and curriculum. Look for courses that cover the topics you're most interested in, whether it's the basics, advanced machine learning techniques, or specific applications like natural language processing. It's also a good idea to check the prerequisites to ensure you have the necessary background knowledge. While some courses require a solid understanding of programming and mathematics, others are designed for beginners.

The format and length of the course are important too. Do you do best with a self-paced course where you can study as and when you like, or do you get on better with a structured environment with deadlines? Reading reviews and testimonials from past students can provide valuable insights into the course's effectiveness and the instructor's teaching style.

Supplementary resources can be incredibly helpful for continuous learning. YouTube channels like "Tech With Tim," "Sentdex," and "3Blue1Brown" offer tutorials and explanations on various AI topics. Blogs and websites such as Towards Data Science and Medium AI publications provide articles and insights from industry experts. Free coding platforms like Codecademy and FreeCodeCamp offer interactive exercises to practice your coding skills, which are essential for implementing AI algorithms.

Engaging with these additional resources can enhance your understanding and keep you updated with the latest developments in AI. Whatever your age or background, these courses and resources are designed to make AI accessible, interesting and enjoyable for everyone.

10.3 AI COMMUNITIES AND FORUMS: FINDING SUPPORT

Exploring the world of AI can feel overwhelming but joining a community can make a significant difference. Online platforms like Reddit are fantastic places to start chatting to like-minded people. Subreddits such as r/MachineLearning and r/ArtificialIntelligence are full of lively discussions ranging from beginner questions to advanced research topics. These forums offer loads of information, where you can read about the latest trends, ask questions and learn from the experiences of others. Whether you're troubleshooting a problem or seeking recommendations for further study, these communities are invaluable.

Stack Overflow is another essential platform, especially for technical queries. The AI and machine learning tags on Stack Overflow are frequented by professionals and enthusiasts who can provide quick detailed answers to your coding and algorithm questions. For instance, if you're stuck on a piece of code for a neural network, a quick search or question on Stack Overflow can often lead to a solution thanks to the collective expertise of its users.

Kaggle offers not only data science competitions but also a thriving community where members share datasets, code and insights. Participating in Kaggle competitions can be an excellent way to apply what you've learned in a practical setting. The community discussions on Kaggle are a great resource for advice on best practices, optimization techniques and innovative approaches to common problems. Engaging with this platform can significantly enhance your practical skills and provide a sense of accomplishment as you solve real-world problems.

The AI Alignment Forum focuses on discussions about AI safety and ethics. Here, you can engage in deep conversations about the implications of AI technologies, explore ethical dilemmas and learn about efforts to ensure that AI development benefits humanity as a whole. This forum is particularly beneficial if you're interested in the broader societal impacts of AI and want to contribute to shaping its future responsibly.

Joining these communities provides several benefits. First, access to diverse perspectives and expertise enriches your understanding of AI. You'll encounter viewpoints and solutions that you might not have considered. Second, these platforms offer opportunities to ask questions and get answers from experienced practitioners, accelerating your learning process. Staying updated with trends and advancements becomes easier when you're part of a community that shares news, research papers and case studies. Networking and collaboration opportunities abound in these spaces where you can talk to like-minded individuals and potential collaborators for projects or research. And at the very least, a lively chat about something that interests you.

To make the most of these communities, start by reading existing posts and discussions. This will give you a sense of the community's tone and the topics that are frequently discussed. When you feel ready, begin participating by asking questions and sharing your insights. Even if you're new to AI, your unique perspective can add value to the conversation. Contributing to open-source projects and competitions is another excellent way to engage. These contributions enhance your skills and build your reputation within the community. Attending virtual meetups and webinars organized by these communities can provide additional learning and networking opportunities.

Community-driven resources and initiatives are invaluable and many forums and platforms curate lists of AI learning materials, making it easier to find high-quality resources. Open-source projects and datasets are often shared within these communities, providing practical tools for learning and experimentation. Collaborative research and development efforts can open doors to new opportunities and partnerships. Mentorship programs and study groups offer personalized guidance and support, helping you get to grips with the intricacies of AI.

Engaging with AI communities and forums can transform your learning experience, providing support, resources and connections that enhance your journey into the world of artificial intelligence.

Whether you're troubleshooting a problem, seeking advice on the best resources, looking to collaborate on a project or an enthusiastic hobbyist, these communities are a mine of knowledge and support to help you thrive in the field of AI.

10.4 MUST-READ BOOKS AND PAPERS ON AI

If you're like me, you'll agree that few things are more relaxing than sitting comfortably in your favorite chair with a great book. In fact, there aren't many better ways to deepen your understanding of AI than through some foundational books that have shaped the field. One such book is "Artificial Intelligence: A Modern Approach" by Stuart Russell and Peter Norvig. This book is often considered the bible of AI, providing a thorough introduction to the theories and applications of artificial intelligence. It covers everything from search algorithms to machine learning, making it a fantastic read for anyone serious about understanding AI.

Another essential read is "Deep Learning" by Ian Goodfellow, Yoshua Bengio, and Aaron Courville. This book delves into the intricacies of deep learning, a subset of machine learning responsible for many recent AI advancements. It covers neural networks, optimization techniques and practical applications, offering both theoretical insights and hands-on examples. This book is a must-read if you want to understand the mechanisms behind deep learning and its real-world applications.

For those interested in the ethical and existential implications of AI, "Superintelligence: Paths, Dangers, Strategies" by Nick Bostrom is a compelling read. Bostrom explores the potential future scenarios where AI surpasses human intelligence and the challenges this poses. He discusses the risks and strategies for ensuring that AI development benefits humanity. This book is thought-provoking and essential for understanding the broader implications of AI technology.

"Life 3.0: Being Human in the Age of Artificial Intelligence" by Max Tegmark is another fascinating book that explores how AI will affect society. Tegmark discusses the impact of AI on jobs, ethics and the future of humanity. He presents a balanced view, highlighting both the opportunities and challenges of AI advancements. The book is accessible and engaging, making complex topics understandable for readers from all backgrounds.

In addition to these books, several research papers have significantly contributed to AI's development. "Attention Is All You Need" by Vaswani et al. introduced the transformer model, revolutionizing natural language processing. This paper laid the groundwork for models like GPT-3, which can generate human-like text with remarkable accuracy. Another landmark paper is "ImageNet Classification with Deep Convolutional Neural Networks" by Krizhevsky et al., which demonstrated the power of deep learning in the context of image recognition. This paper showed how convolutional neural networks could achieve unprecedented accuracy in visual tasks.

"Playing Atari with Deep Reinforcement Learning" by Mnih et al. is another influential paper that showcases the potential of reinforcement learning. The researchers trained a neural network to play Atari games at a superhuman level, demonstrating the power of combining deep learning with reinforcement learning. Lastly, "Generative Adversarial Nets" by Goodfellow et al. introduced GANs, a framework for generating realistic images. GANs have since been used in various applications, from image synthesis to data augmentation.

Keeping up with AI literature is great for continuous learning as new research and advancements crop up regularly, pushing the boundaries of what's possible. Staying educated will make sure you continue to increase your understanding of the latest processes and advancements thus keeping you at the forefront of the field. Understanding the evolution and ethics of AI helps you appreciate the progress made and the challenges ahead.

When reading and analyzing AI literature, start by skimming the abstract and conclusion to get an overview of the paper's main points. Focus on the methodology and results sections for technical details, as these provide insight into how the research was conducted and its outcomes. Take notes and summarize key points to reinforce your understanding. Discussing and sharing insights with peers or in study groups can further deepen your comprehension and provide different perspectives on the material.

Engaging with these books and papers will enrich your knowledge and understanding of AI, making you well-equipped to navigate this fascinating field.

10.5 AI CONFERENCES AND WORKSHOPS: EXPANDING YOUR KNOWLEDGE

Imagine the excitement of attending a major AI conference, where the brightest minds in the field gather to share their latest research and innovations. One of the most influential events is NeurIPS (Neural Information Processing Systems). This conference focuses on machine learning and computational neuroscience, attracting researchers and practitioners from around the world. The presentations and workshops cover a wide range of topics, from deep learning to reinforcement learning, providing an extensive view of current trends and future directions in AI.

Another key event is the International Conference on Machine Learning (ICML). ICML is well known for its rigorous peer-reviewed papers and high-quality workshops. The conference covers various aspects of machine learning, including algorithms, theory and applications. Attending ICML offers a unique opportunity to learn about cutting-edge research and network with experts.

The Conference on Computer Vision and Pattern Recognition (CVPR) is a must-attend event for those interested in computer vision. It showcases the latest advancements in image and video analysis, object detection, and visual recognition. The event includes tutorials, technical sessions, and poster presentations, providing a rich learning experience.

The Association for the Advancement of Artificial Intelligence (AAAI) conference covers a broad spectrum of AI topics, from natural language processing to robotics. AAAI aims to promote research in AI and foster collaboration among researchers, practitioners and educators. The conference features keynote speakers, panel discussions and workshops, offering valuable insights into the ethical and societal implications of AI.

Attending AI conferences provides numerous benefits. You gain access to cutting-edge research and presentations, learning about the latest discoveries and technological advancements. These events also offer unparalleled networking opportunities. You can connect with AI experts, researchers and peers, exchanging ideas and forging collaborations. Exposure to new tools, technologies and methodologies can inspire and motivate you to explore new directions in your work. Keynote speakers and panel discussions often provide thought-provoking insights, sparking new ideas and perspectives.

To make the most of AI conferences, plan and schedule your sessions. Read the conference program and choose the sessions that align with your interests and goals. Get the very best from your experience by engaging with presenters and asking questions as well as participating in discussions. This will be invaluable in deepening your understanding and give valuable feedback. To enhance your learning even more, take advantage of workshops and hands-on sessions to gain practical experience with new tools and techniques. Follow up with contacts you meet at the conference, continuing discussions and exploring potential collaborations.

If you can't attend in person, many conferences have virtual and online options. Live-streamed sessions and webinars mean you can participate remotely, accessing the same high-quality content. Recorded presentations and materials provide the flexibility to learn at your own speed. Virtual networking events and discussion forums enable you to connect with other attendees, from wherever you are. Online workshops and tutorials offer interactive learning experiences, ensuring you can still gain practical skills and knowledge.

In conclusion, AI conferences and workshops are invaluable for expanding your knowledge, staying updated with the latest advancements, and connecting with the AI community. By actively participating and utilizing both in-person and virtual options, you can maximize the benefits of these events and continue to grow in your AI journey.

11

THE FUTURE OF AI

By now, it'll be easy for you to imagine a world where AI enhances your morning routine. Preparing for the day, an AI assistant updates you with personalized news and weather forecasts. Your smart home adjusts the temperature, and your fridge suggests breakfast options based on your dietary needs and what's available. Sounds like science fiction, doesn't it? But it's not. It's a glimpse of how AI will shape our everyday lives. Let's look at the profound implications of AI on society and explore both its potential benefits and challenges.

11.1 AI AND SOCIETY: POTENTIAL IMPACTS AND CHANGES

AI's role in addressing social issues is increasingly significant. These days, AI can be a game-changer in disaster response and management. This can solve the problems that traditional methods have with handling emergencies, often struggling with resource allocation and situational awareness. AI can process large amounts of data in real time, optimizing emergency services and resource deployment. For example during wildfires, AI can analyze satellite images to predict fire spread so that firefighters can act swiftly and effectively. Similarly, in the aftermath of natural disasters like hurricanes or earthquakes, AI can assess damage using aerial imagery, speeding up relief efforts so that aid reaches the most affected areas promptly.

Beyond crisis management, AI-driven initiatives are making strides in poverty alleviation and food security. In developing countries, AI is used to identify optimal locations for renewable energy sources, bringing electricity to remote areas. By analyzing data on wind patterns and solar radiation, AI helps set up sustainable energy infrastructure, improving the quality of life for millions. Additionally, AI technologies like computer vision and predictive analytics are revolutionizing agriculture. Tools such as FarmView employ robotics and machine learning to optimize crop growth, enhancing yields and resource efficiency. In areas where farming is a major source of income, these advancements make a massive contribution to reducing poverty.

The role of AI in public safety and crime prevention is well documented. Law enforcement agencies increasingly use AI to predict and prevent criminal activities, and AI systems analyze crime data to identify patterns and hotspots, enabling proactive measures. Not only can predictive policing algorithms forecast where crimes are likely to occur, but also AI-driven surveillance systems with facial recognition can track suspects in real-time to increase public safety. However, these applications raise significant ethical and privacy concerns that need careful consideration, and errors in facial recognition systems have been known to result in wrongful arrests and imprisonment.

The integration of AI into society is not without risks. Job displacement and economic inequality are critical challenges.

Privacy matters and data security are crucial as AI systems become more knowledgeable about individuals. AI's ability to analyze personal data for insights raises questions about how this information is used and protected. There needs to be reassurance that AI applications comply with data protection laws and that user privacy is maintained. Moreover, there's the potential for bias in AI decision-making to pose significant ethical dilemmas. There needs to be transparent and fair AI algorithms to mitigate these risks.

AI's influence extends to human relationships and communication with social media platforms driven by AI algorithms shaping how we interact and consume information. These platforms personalize content, keeping users engaged but also creating echo chambers that reinforce existing beliefs. AI's role in curating content raises concerns about misinformation and polarization. Additionally, virtual companions powered by AI are emerging as tools to combat loneliness, particularly among the elderly. These companions, capable of engaging in meaningful conversations, offer emotional support and companionship. In mental health, AI-driven chatbots and virtual therapists provide accessible counseling services, offering support to those who may not seek traditional therapy.

Public awareness and education about AI are vital for its responsible integration into society. Promoting AI literacy ensures that individuals understand how AI works and its potential impacts. Knowledge, as they say, is power, enabling people to use AI responsibly and make informed decisions about its applications. Encouraging responsible AI use involves fostering digital citizenship, where individuals are mindful of ethical considerations and data privacy. Integrating AI education into school curricula prepares future generations to navigate an AI-driven world. Teaching students about AI principles, ethics and practical applications equips them with the skills needed for the evolving job market.

Reflection Exercise: How Do You See AI Impacting Your Life?

Take a moment to reflect on how AI might influence your daily life. Consider areas such as your job, interactions with technology and personal relationships. Write down your thoughts and any concerns or hopes you have about living in an AI-driven world. This exercise will help you engage more deeply with the material and think critically about AI's role in your life.

11.2 ENCOURAGEMENT FOR FUTURE EXPLORATION: THE JOURNEY AHEAD

Curiosity is the engine that drives discovery. As you are already discovering, staying curious is your best asset in the dynamic world of AI. AI is not static. In fact it evolves constantly. Every day, new algorithms emerge, new applications are discovered and new ethical challenges arise, and it is this ever-changing landscape that makes AI such an exciting field to explore. It's essential to keep yourself educated to make sure you are keeping up with these advancements. Think of AI as a river, always flowing and changing its course. To navigate it successfully, you must continue to learn and adapt. Remember that you can always deepen your knowledge through continuous education via courses, workshops and confer-ences. Additionally, there is no shortage of podcasts on various AI topics. Search on your favorite podcast platforms, and you will be spoiled for choice.

Interdisciplinary collaboration is vital for innovative AI solutions. Combining AI with fields like biology, environmental science and humanities can lead to groundbreaking discoveries. For instance, AI algorithms can analyze biological data to predict disease outbreaks or optimize agricultural practices. In environmental science, AI can monitor climate change patterns and suggest mitigation strategies.

Collaborating with experts from different disciplines brings diverse perspectives to the table, enriching the problem-solving process. An exciting example of this is working on projects that combine AI and art to create stunning visualizations. These visualizations can communicate complex data in an accessible way, bridging the gap between technical insights and visual comprehension. Successful interdisciplinary AI collaborations are already making waves. Consider the project where AI and biology intersect to combat diseases. AI algorithms analyze genetic data to identify potential treatments, accelerating drug discovery. In another example, AI and environmental science collaborate to monitor deforestation using satellite imagery, providing real-time data to conservationists. These collaborations highlight the immense potential of AI when combined with other fields. They also emphasize the importance of teamwork and diverse skill sets in tackling complex problems.

AI has the potential to be a tool for positive global change and innovation. There is so much that can be done. There are AI systems that predict and prevent diseases. And what about the AI-driven solutions that optimize resource use, reduce waste, and promote sustainability? Just think about the endless possibility of AI applications that enhance human capabilities, allowing us to achieve feats previously thought impossible. The fascinating thing about the future of AI is that it's not just about technology but also what AI can achieve to create a better world.

Stories of pioneers and innovators in the AI field are abundant. Take, for instance, the work of Fei-Fei Li, a leading figure in computer vision. Her contributions have significantly advanced the field, enabling machines to interpret and understand visual data. Or consider Demis Hassabis, co-founder of DeepMind, whose team's AI, AlphaGo, defeated a world champion in the complex game of Go. The problem-solving skills of AlphaGo were just mind-boggling. These pioneers are not just pushing the boundaries of AI; they are shaping its future, demonstrating its potential and inspiring the next generation of AI enthusiasts.

Reflecting on these stories, it's clear that the journey of learning and exploring AI is both challenging and rewarding. The vast field has endless opportunities to innovate and make a difference. Whatever the reason for your pursuit of knowledge in the field of AI, the key is to stay curious, keep learning and embrace the dynamic nature of AI. It's a field where imagination meets technology, creating ideas that were once considered unrealistic. As you continue to explore AI, remember that each discovery, each new skill and each collaboration contributes to the broader tapestry of innovation and progress.

11.3 PREDICTING THE FUTURE: AI IN THE NEXT DECADE

The next decade promises cutting-edge advancements in AI technology that will revolutionize our lives. One significant area of development is in AI algorithms and models. Researchers are continually refining algorithms to be more efficient and accurate. For example, advancements in deep learning and neural networks will enable AI systems to process and analyze data faster and more accurately. This means AI could identify complex patterns and make predictions with unprecedented precision, impacting fields like healthcare, finance, and beyond.

An exciting prospect is the increased amalgamation of AI with technologies like the Internet of Things (IoT) and blockchain. IoT devices, embedded with sensors and connected to the internet, collect large volumes of data. When combined with AI, this data can be analyzed in real time to optimize various processes. For instance, in smart cities (think London, New York, and Berlin, for example) AI can manage traffic flow by analyzing data from connected vehicles and traffic lights, reducing congestion and improving safety. Similarly, blockchain technology can provide secure and transparent data transactions, enhancing the reliability of AI systems in sectors like finance and supply chain management.

AI-human interaction interfaces are also set to become more sophisticated. Virtual assistants understanding and responding to human emotions are set to become a reality. With advancements in natural language processing and machine learning, these interfaces will become more intuitive and responsive. This could revolutionize customer service, making interactions more personalized and efficient. Additionally, AI-driven virtual reality environments could provide immersive experiences for education, training, and entertainment, blurring the lines between the digital and physical worlds.

The impact of AI on various industries will be profound. In further healthcare innovations, AI-driven precision medicine will recommend treatments for individual patients based on their genetic makeup and lifestyle. This approach will improve treatment outcomes and reduce side effects. AI-enabled virtual healthcare will provide remote consultations and monitoring, making healthcare more accessible, especially in underserved areas. We already inhabit a world where your smartwatch continuously monitors your health. How amazing when it can alert your doctor to any potential issues before they become serious. This proactive approach could save your life and reduce healthcare costs.

In education, AI will create personalized learning experiences. AI tutors will adapt to each student's learning style and pace, providing customized support and feedback. This individualized attention benefits students enormously, helping them to grasp complex concepts and stay engaged in their studies. A school where each pupil has a virtual teacher that identifies their strengths and weaknesses and tailors lessons to their needs has got to be a good thing. This could ultimately level the education playing field so that there will be a vast improvement in equal learning opportunities for all students regardless of their background.

Transportation will also see significant transformations. Fully autonomous vehicles will become more common, reducing the need for human drivers and potentially lowering accident rates. A driverless taxi system developed by Google, called Waymo is already operating in San Francisco. Smart traffic management systems powered by AI will optimize traffic flow, reduce congestion and minimize environmental impact. Not so very far into the future, we can look forward to a time when self-driving cars interact with each other and traffic infrastructure to find the most efficient routes. This could lead to benefits such as less stressful commutes, reduced pollution and safer roads.

Agriculture will benefit from AI-powered precision farming and crop monitoring. AI systems will analyze data from drones and sensors to optimize irrigation, fertilization, and pest control. Crop yields can be increased and waste reduced, making farming more sustainable. AI will also be useful for weather predictions and based on the information provided, farming practices can be adjusted accordingly. This will increase the probability of better harvests and diminish the effect of climate change on agriculture.

As AI advances, ethical and regulatory considerations will become increasingly important. The introduction of global AI ethics standards will influence the development of AI systems and the way they are used, increasing the likelihood that they are fair, transparent, and accountable. Ethical AI certifications and compliance requirements will ensure that AI systems meet high ethical standards. These measures will address concerns about bias, privacy, and accountability, fostering trust in AI technologies.

Societal changes driven by AI will reshape our daily lives. Enhanced accessibility and inclusivity through AI innovations will empower individuals with disabilities, providing tools that support independence and improve quality of life. For instance, AI-powered assistive devices could enable people with visual impairments to navigate their environments more easily.

AI will also be important in addressing global challenges like climate change and poverty. AI systems can analyze vast amounts of environmental data to predict and reduce the effects of climate change. By optimizing resource use and developing sustainable practices, AI can contribute to environmental conservation. Additionally, AI-driven initiatives for poverty alleviation will provide innovative solutions to improve living conditions and economic opportunities for disadvantaged communities.

These are exciting times. AI will enhance efficiency and productivity in the coming decade and transform how we live, work, and interact with the world. As these advancements unfold, it is essential to stay informed while observing how AI technologies can benefit society in general. By embracing AI's potential and addressing its challenges, we can create a future where technology enhances human capabilities and improves the quality of life for all.

CONCLUSION

Let's wrap up by looking back at how far we've come.

From the basics of AI, through various applications, a few technical details, and plenty of ethical considerations. I've included some practical exercises to give some context. There's so much more to all this and I hope that reading this book has given you the incentive to keep digging.

The intention of writing this book has been to transform AI from a subject of suspicion into a compelling interest in a way that makes it relevant to you. I wanted to show you that AI is not just for tech experts but for everyone. AI has something to offer whoever you are, and whatever your background or age. An amazing catalyst for innovation across industries, sparking new ideas and approaches, it is a subject that can easily evolve into a lifelong interest.

You now possess the foundational knowledge and resources to explore AI further. The world of AI is huge, and I think it's safe to say there will always be more to discover. It's worth remembering that every expert was once a beginner, so it makes sense to keep up with exploring, experimenting, and learning at your own pace.

From here, I encourage you to take the next steps in your AI journey. Start a small project using what you've learned. Join an AI community to share your experiences and learn from others. Stay updated by reading, attending conferences, and taking online courses. And above all, keep asking questions and then more questions after that. Look for help any time you need to, there's plenty to be had.

As AI continues to evolve, your journey of understanding has only just begun. I hope this book inspires you to stay enthusiastic, curious and engaged in shaping the future of this trailblazing technology.

KEEPING THE AI JOURNEY ALIVE

You've reached the finish line—well done on completing your journey into AI.

By now, you have everything you need to understand the fundamentals of this complex yet fascinating subject, and now it's time to share your knowledge and help others on their path.

By leaving your honest opinion of *The Essentials of AI for Beginners* on Amazon, you'll guide other readers, just like you to the information they've been searching for. Your review can spark someone else's curiosity and help them discover the exciting world of AI.

Thank you for your support. By writing a review, you're empowering the AI learning community—feeding curiosity and helping others explore this exciting territory.

Your voice matters—I'd be grateful if you took a moment to share your thoughts in a review.

It truly makes a difference.

It's easy. All you have to do is scan the QR code here to leave your review on Amazon.

Thank you for your support. By writing a review, you're empowering the AI learning community—feeding curiosity and helping others explore this exciting territory.

GLOSSARY

Algorithm: A set of rules or step-by-step instructions computers use to perform tasks, such as solving problems or making decisions.

Artificial Intelligence (AI): The simulation of human intelligence by machines, allowing them to learn, reason, and perform tasks typically requiring human intelligence.

Bias in AI: This occurs when AI systems produce results that reflect biases found in the data they were trained on, often leading to unfair or unbalanced outcomes.

Big Data: Extremely large datasets that are too complex for traditional data processing methods but can be analyzed using AI and machine learning techniques.

Chatbot: An AI program that simulates human conversation, often used in customer service or online help systems.

Computer Vision: A field of AI that enables computers to interpret and understand the visual world. Using digital images or video, computer vision systems can identify objects, analyze scenes, and make decisions based on visual data.

Data: Raw information, such as numbers, text, images, or sound, that can be processed and analyzed by computers to make decisions.

Data Mining: The process of discovering patterns and useful information from large datasets using statistical techniques and machine learning.

Deep Learning: A subset of machine learning where neural networks with many layers learn from large amounts of data to recognize patterns and make decisions.

Ethics in AI: The principles that guide the development and use of AI, ensuring that AI technologies are created and used responsibly, fairly, and safely.

Machine Learning (ML): A subset of AI in which computers use algorithms to learn and improve from experience without being explicitly programmed automatically.

Model: In AI, a model is the mathematical representation of a real-world process or problem. AI models are trained using data to make predictions or decisions.

Natural Language Processing (NLP): A field of AI focused on the interaction between computers and humans through natural language. It involves teaching computers to understand, interpret, and generate human language.

Neural Network: A type of machine learning model inspired by the structure and function of the human brain, consisting of interconnected nodes (neurons) that process data.

Overfitting: A modeling error in machine learning where a model performs well on training data but fails to generalize to new, unseen data.

Prompts: The input instructions or queries provided to an AI model to guide its response

Reinforcement Learning: A type of machine learning where an agent learns by interacting with its environment, receiving rewards or penalties based on its actions.

Regression Tasks: A type of supervised learning problem where the goal is to predict a continuous value (e.g., predicting house prices, temperature, or stock prices). In regression tasks, the model learns from labeled examples where the output variable is a numerical value, and it attempts to minimize the difference between its predictions and the actual target values.

Stemming: A process in language processing where words are reduced to their base or root form. For example, "running," "runner," and "ran" can be reduced to the stem "run." This helps computers understand different forms of a word as being related, which is useful in search engines and text analysis

Strong AI: A theoretical form of AI that possesses general intelligence, meaning it can understand, learn, and apply knowledge in a way similar to human intelligence.

Supervised Learning: A type of machine learning where a model is trained on labeled data, meaning that the desired output is provided for each input during training.

Tokenization: The process of breaking down text into smaller units, called tokens, such as words, phrases, or characters, which are used as input for AI models. Removing stop words, which are common words that don't add much meaning, like "the" or "and."

Unsupervised Learning: A type of machine learning where the model learns from unlabeled data, identifying patterns and relationships without predefined answers.

Weak AI: Also known as narrow AI, it refers to AI systems designed to perform a specific task or set of tasks but lack general intelligence.

REFERENCES

Akkio. (2024, January). The complete no-code AI guide (Updated January 2024). https://www.akkio.com/post/no-code-ai-tools-complete-guide

Analytics Vidhya. (2021, June). Image processing using CNN: A beginners guide. https://www.analyticsvidhya.com/blog/2021/06/image-processing-using-cnn-a-beginners-guide/

Analytics Vidhya. (2021, April). Probability theory basics in machine learning. https://www.analyticsvidhya.com/blog/2021/04/probability-theory-basics-in-machine-learning/

Augmented Startups. (n.d.). 5 real-world applications of deep learning. https://www.augmentedstartups.com/blog/5-real-world-applications-of-deep-learning

Built In. (n.d.). PyTorch vs. TensorFlow for deep learning. https://builtin.com/data-science/pytorch-vs-tensorflow

Deloitte. (n.d.). Leveraging AI in emergency management and crisis response. https://www2.deloitte.com/us/en/insights/industry/public-sector/automation-and-generative-ai-in-government/leveraging-ai-in-emergency-management-and-crisis-response.html

Developers For Hire. (2024). Find & hire AI engineers: 15 best sites [2024]. https://www.developersforhire.com/ai

Dialzara. (n.d.). Privacy-preserving AI: Techniques & frameworks. https://dialzara.com/blog/privacy-preserving-ai-techniques-and-frameworks/

Discover Magazine. (n.d.). AI and the human brain: How similar are they? https://www.discovermagazine.com/technology/ai-and-the-human-brain-how-similar-are-they

Ethics of AI. (n.d.). A framework for AI ethics. MOOC.fi. https://ethics-of-ai.mooc.fi/chapter-1/4-a-framework-for-ai-ethics/

Forbes. (2023, May 10). 15 amazing real-world applications of AI everyone should know about. https://www.forbes.com/sites/bernardmarr/2023/05/10/15-amazing-real-world-applications-of-ai-everyone-should-know-about/

GetCoAI. (n.d.). AI-powered Nest thermostat learns faster, saves more energy. https://getcoai.com/news/ai-powered-nest-thermostat-learns-faster-saves-more-energy/

Google Cloud. (n.d.). 101 real-world gen AI use cases from the world's leading companies. https://cloud.google.com/transform/101-real-world-generative-ai-use-cases-from-industry-leaders

Google Cloud. (n.d.). Explainable AI. https://cloud.google.com/explainable-ai

Grammarly. (n.d.). How to create effective AI prompts (With examples). https://www.grammarly.com/blog/generative-ai-prompts/

Harvard Gazette. (2020, October 26). Ethical concerns mount as AI takes bigger decision-making role. https://news.harvard.edu/gazette/story/2020/10/ethical-concerns-mount-as-ai-takes-bigger-decision-making-role/

How to Learn Machine Learning. (n.d.). Narrow AI vs general AI and super AI: How do they differ? https://howtolearnmachinelearning.com/articles/narrow-ai-vs-general-ai/

IBM. (n.d.). Supervised vs. unsupervised learning. https://www.ibm.com/think/topics/supervised-vs-unsupervised-learning

Information Week. (n.d.). Quantum computing and AI: A perfect match? https://www.informationweek.com/machine-learning-ai/quantum-computing-and-ai-a-perfect-match-

Innopharma Education. (n.d.). The impact of AI on job roles, workforce, and employment. https://www.innopharmaeducation.com/our-blog/the-impact-of-ai-on-job-roles-workforce-and-employment-what-you-need-to-know

Kasma, A. (2024). SageMaker Studio Lab vs Google Colab: A comprehensive comparison for 2024. Medium. https://medium.com/@ashukasma/sagemaker-studio-lab-vs-google-colab-a-comprehensive-comparison-for-2024-cc812696f1a1

Learn Data Science. (2024). The 9 best AI courses online for 2024: Beginner to advanced. https://www.learndatasci.com/best-artificial-intelligence-ai-courses/

Lewis C. Lin. (n.d.). Diagnosing and troubleshooting your AI prompts: A comprehensive checklist. https://www.lewis-lin.com/blog/diagnosing-and-troubleshooting-your-ai-prompts-a-comprehensive-checklist

LinkedIn. (n.d.). AI for A/B testing: How artificial intelligence optimizes your experiments. https://www.linkedin.com/pulse/ai-ab-testing-how-artificial-intelligence-optimizes-your-mayank-deo

LinkedIn. (n.d.). Tips to manage and motivate learners in self-paced training. https://www.linkedin.com/advice/0/how-do-you-manage-motivate-learners-self-paced

Magical. (n.d.). How to write good AI prompts: A beginner's guide (+12 examples). https://www.getmagical.com/blog/how-to-write-good-ai-prompts

Marqo. (n.d.). Getting started with Google Colab: A beginner's guide. https://www.marqo.ai/blog/getting-started-with-google-colab-a-beginners-guide

McKinsey & Company. (2023). The state of AI in 2023: Generative AI's breakout year. https://www.mckinsey.com/capabilities/quantumblack/our-insights/the-state-of-ai-in-2023-generative-ais-breakout-year

MDPI. (n.d.). Fairness and bias in artificial intelligence: A brief survey of sources, manifestations, and mitigation strategies. https://www.mdpi.com/2413-4155/6/1/3

Medium. (n.d.). AI in business: Real-world case studies. https://medium.com/@trienpont/ai-in-business-real-world-case-studies-85c9d923c90a

Medium. (n.d.). Case study: How Netflix uses AI to personalize content recommendations and improve digital experience. https://medium.com/@shizk/case-study-how-netflix-uses-ai-to-personalize-content-recommendations-and-improve-digital-b253d08352fd

Moluguri, V. K. (n.d.). Google's Teachable Machine AI: Step-by-step tutorial included. Medium. https://vinaykumarmoluguri.medium.com/googles-teachable-machine-ai-step-by-step-tutorial-included-6a7200199932

NASA. (n.d.). Artificial intelligence. https://www.nasa.gov/artificial-intelligence/

NIST. (n.d.). Alan Turing's everlasting contributions to computing, AI and cryptography. https://www.nist.gov/blogs/taking-measure/alan-turings-everlasting-contributions-computing-ai-and-cryptography

Real Python. (n.d.). ChatterBot: Build a chatbot with Python. https://realpython.com/build-a-chatbot-python-chatterbot/

Real Python. (n.d.). How to install Python on your system: A guide. https://realpython.com/installing-python/

Simplilearn. (n.d.). Artificial intelligence job description: Skills | Roles. https://www.simplilearn.com/artificial-intelligence-job-description-article

STAT. (2018, August 13). Google DeepMind AI system diagnoses eye diseases and shows its work. https://www.statnews.com/2018/08/13/google-deepmind-ai-diagnoses-eye-diseases/

Superior Data Science. (n.d.). J.P Morgan – COiN – a case study of AI in finance. https://superiordatascience.com/jp-morgan-coin-a-case-study-of-ai-in-finance/

Tableau. (n.d.). 14 of the best books about artificial intelligence (AI). https://www.tableau.com/learn/articles/books-about-artificial-intelligence

TechTarget. (n.d.). The future of AI: What to expect in the next 5 years. https://www.techtarget.com/searchenterpriseai/tip/The-future-of-AI-What-to-expect-in-the-next-5-years

TechTarget. (n.d.). What is the Turing Test? https://www.techtarget.com/searchenterpriseai/definition/Turing-test

Towards Data Science. (n.d.). Netflix recommender system — A big data case study.

https://towardsdatascience.com/netflix-recommender-system-a-big-data-case-study-19cfa6d56ff5

2slash.ai. (2023). Top 12 AI communities to join in 2023. https://2s-lash.ai/blog/top-ai-communities-2023/

UCL Pi Media. (n.d.). Byte by byte: How AI is revolutionising poverty alleviation efforts. https://uclpimedia.com/online/byte-by-byte-how-ai-is-revolutionis-ing-poverty-alleviation-efforts

Upwork. (n.d.). 10 AI jobs for non-techies: Work with AI, not code. https://www.upwork.com/resources/ai-jobs-for-non-techies

360Learning. (n.d.). Reskilling reinvented: Top 10 AI-powered learning platforms. https://360learning.com/blog/ai-learning-platforms/

Printed in Dunstable, United Kingdom